Gypsy Dream Secrets Revealed

You are flying through fog, when suddenly you see a boy in an apple tree, playing a violin. He hands you a red apple, and smiles. What is this dream telling you?

The dream world has its own language; a visual and symbolic language, filled with obscure clues and hidden meanings. Learn how to accurately decipher your dream experiences, using centuries-old Gypsy folk wisdom. *Gypsy Dream Dictionary* contains over 850 dream symbols to help you uncover the messeges in your dreams.

What is lucid dreaming? What is false awakening? How can you experience prophetic dreams or astral travel? *Gypsy Dream Dictionary* answers these questions and more. You will learn the secrets of the dream world, secrets which will enable you to better understand this realm and even direct your dream experiences.

With this valuable book as your guide, your nightly excursions into the land of dreams can be exciting and satisfying journeys of discovery and adventure.

About the Author

Ray Buckland's grandfather was the first of the Buckland Gypsies to give up traveling the roads in wagons and to settle in a permanent house. From his earliest years Ray remembers listening to his father's and grandfather's tales of Romani life and watching his grandmother read cards and tell fortunes. "Buckland" is a well-known name among English Gypsies, and Ray Buckland has become a well-known author of books on practical magic. He is today regarded as one of the leading authorities on witchcraft, voodoo, and the supernatural.

To Write to the Author

If you wish to contact the author or would like more information about this book, please write to the author in care of Llewellyn Worldwide, and we will forward your request. Both the author and publisher appreciate hearing from you and learning of your enjoyment of this book and how it has helped you. Llewellyn Worldwide cannot guarantee that every letter written to the author can be answered, but all will be forwarded. Please write:

Raymond Buckland
c/o Llewellyn Worldwide
P.O. Box 64383, K090-6
St. Paul, MN 55164-0383, U.S.A.

Please enclose a self-addressed, stamped envelope for reply, or $1.00 to cover costs. If outside the U.S.A., enclose international postal reply coupon.

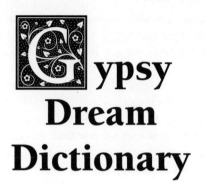

Gypsy
Dream
Dictionary

Raymond Buckland

2003
Llewellyn Publications
St. Paul, Minnesota, 55164-0383, U.S.A.

SECOND EDITION
Fourth printing, 2003
(previously titled *Secrets of Gypsy Dream Reading*)

First edition, 1990

Cover design: Anne Marie Garrison
Second edition book design and project management: Christine Snow
Second edition book layout: Virginia Sutton

Library of Congress Cataloging-in-Publication Data
Buckland, Raymond.
      Gypsy dream dictionary / Raymond Buckland. -- 2nd ed.
        p.   cm.
      Rev. ed. of: Secrets of Gypsy dream reading.
      Includes index.
      ISBN 1-56718-090-6
      1. Dreams. 2. Dreams--Dictionaries. 3. Gypsies--Miscellanea.
  I. Buckland, Raymond. Secrets of Gypsy dream reading. II. Title.
BF1091.B89   1999
135'.3'08991497--dc21   98–31529
                                        CIP

Llewellyn Worldwide does not participate in, endorse, or have any authority or responsibility concerning private business transactions between our authors and the public.

    All mail addressed to the author is forwarded but the publisher cannot, unless specifically instructed by the author, give out an address or phone number. The publisher has not tested the techniques included in this book, and takes no position on their effectiveness.

Llewellyn Publications
A Division of Llewellyn Worldwide, Ltd.
P.O. Box 64383, St. Paul, MN 55164-0383
www.llewellyn.com

Printed in the United States of America

Other Books by Raymond Buckland

Llewellyn Publications

Gypsy Witchcraft and Magic (1998)

Gypsy Fortune Telling Tarot Kit (book and deck, 1998)

Advanced Candle Magick (1996)

Cardinal's Sin (fiction, 1996)

Buckland Gypsies' Domino Divination Deck (1995)

Truth About Spirit Communication (1995)

The Committee (fiction, 1993)

Doors to Other Worlds (1993)

Scottish Witchcraft (1991)

Secrets of Gypsy Love Magick (1990)

Witchcraft Yesterday and Today (video, 1990)

Secrets of Gypsy Fortunetelling (1988)

Buckland's Complete Book of Witchcraft (1986)

Color Magick (*formerly* Practical Color Magick) (1983, 2002)

Witchcraft from the Inside (1971, 1975, 1995)

Practical Candleburning Rituals (1970, 1976, 1982)

Coin Divination (2000)

The Buckland Romani Tarot (2001)

Other Publishers

Ray Buckland's Magic Cauldron (Galde Press, 1995)

The Book of African Divination (Inner Traditions, 1992) *with Kathleen Binger*

The Magic of Chant-O-Matics (Parker, 1978)
Anatomy of the Occult (Weiser, 1977)
Amazing Secrets of the Psychic World (Parker, 1975)
    with Hereward Carrington
Here Is the Occult (HC, 1974)
The Tree: Complete Book of Saxon Witchcraft
    (Weiser, 1974)
Mu Revealed (Warner Paperback Library, 1970)
    under the pseudonym "Tony Earll"
Witchcraft Ancient and Modern (HC, 1970)
A Pocket Guide to the Supernatural (Ace, 1969)
Witchcraft . . . the Religion (Buckland Museum, 1966)

Contents

Gypsies are not especially aware of the necessity but they do know that, of the many people who do dream, there are a vast number who do not understand the meaning of what they dream. Indeed, probably the majority of dreamers do not understand the meaning of what they experience. Gypsies believe that dreams are special knowledge that is being presented to us by our ancestors. It is knowledge that can benefit us, if we recognize it and use it.

The interpretation of dreams has always held a fascination for people and many books have been written on the subject. My earlier edition of this book, titled *Secrets of Gypsy Dream Reading,* showed that the Gypsy interpretations are especially respected. The Romani (Rom) have, for generations, led a nomadic existence and, in their travels, have amassed a wealth of information pertaining to dreams and they take them very seriously. Many people will confide in a Gypsy stranger even more than they might in a medical professional, when it comes to the details of what they have dreamed. In this way, the Rom have been able to put their finger on many little nuances that are found in these nighttime revelations. They have become the "interpreters supreme" when it comes to dreams.

Time does not stand still, even for such tradition-bound people as the Rom. *Vardos*—the old horse-drawn wagons—have given way to more modern mobile homes and trailers, many with television sets installed. Some Gypsies have even started using computers! It is not surprising, then, that they have also kept up to date on their dream interpretation.

In this new edition of the book, now titled *Gypsy Dream Dictionary,* I have expanded to include such dream symbolism as computers, television, movies, and the like. Yet even with modern techno-dreams, the Gypsies seem to have more of a handle on dream reading than does anyone else. The interpretations found in this book are far more accurate, much closer to true meanings, than may be found in the majority of dream books.

My research into the Gypsy way of life has been ongoing, as may be seen in my recent book *Gypsy Witchcraft and Magic* (Llewellyn, 1998), and has always included probing the Rom interpretation of dreams. To my mind they are the best interpreters of this fascinating and little understood aspect of our lives.

—September 1998

Chapter 1

The Inner World of the Dream

The Babylonian *Epic of Gilgamesh*, one of the oldest known texts dating from about 4,000 years ago, is filled with dreams, dream imagery, and interpretation. Egyptian papyrus scrolls on the interpretation of dreams date back to 2000 BCE. In Assyria, in the royal library of King Assurbanipal (c. 650

1

BCE), there were clay tablets covered with dream symbol interpretation.

Dreams, although still a mystery to humankind, are commonplace enough today to be accepted without question. Everyone dreams. Some people rarely remember their dreams but they do have them. In fact, if we did not have dreams, it is believed that we would go mad. We do not, however, dream from the moment we fall asleep until the time we wake up. We dream perhaps five to seven times a night, at intervals of about an hour.

The Egyptian Thothmes IV (1425-1408 BCE), before he became Pharaoh, dreamed that the sun god Harmakhis appeared to him and told him to remove the sand that had piled up against the Sphinx (the head of the Sphinx is a representation of Harmakhis, a form of Ra). As soon as Thothmes ascended the throne, he did just that, believing that the god really had spoken to him. It has long been believed that dreams are not simply nighttime images of no consequence, but are important messages, regardless of where we might believe they originate.

An unknown Jewish writer of the third century said that a dream is like an unread letter. Indeed, the modern view is that a dream is a letter to oneself. But is it "to one-self" (in other words originating internally) or is it from someone else; from some external source?

In the Gilgamesh epic there are the lines:

> They dug a ditch facing the Sun god.
> Gilgamesh stood on the slope of the ditch and
> poured flour into it, saying:
> "Oh, mountain! Bring us dreams!"

Dreams, then, have long been sought as signs and portents of the future.

In the second century BCE there were over three hundred temples scattered throughout Greece and other Mediterranean lands dedicated to Aesculapius and devoted to inducing prophetic dreams. These were usually dreams dealing with the healing of afflictions suffered by the dreamer. A patient could go to a temple and there go through a period of ritual fasting and cleansing before sleeping. Then, through dreams, he or she would receive from the god the key to the cure for the ailment. Initially, dreams were sought to bring answers to a wide variety of personal questions and problems, but rapidly the dreamers became focused on health problems.

Aristotle wrote three essays on dreams but did not believe that they were messages from the gods.

The Roman soothsayer Artemidorus was probably the first to compile and circulate a dream dictionary, written in the second century CE. It was titled *Oneirocritica*, literally meaning "dream judging." It was translated into English as *The Interpretation of Dreames* in 1644.[1] Artemidorus spent many years traveling around Greece and other areas, visiting the dream temples and talking with dream interpreters. He distinguished five different types of dreams: prophetic, symbolic, fantasies, nightmares, and daydreams. From his studies, he proclaimed that dreams could not be interpreted without considering the dreamer's personality and circumstances, and that individual symbols must be viewed in context with the complete dream.

Many primitives treat dreams with great respect. For example, the Senoi of the Malay Peninsula interpret their dreams as an important part of their daily lives. Senoi children are encouraged to recall details of their dreams and to search them for anything that can contribute to the tribe's

---

1. The science or art of dream interpretation is sometimes termed "oneiromancy."

cultural life: a story, poem, dance, or idea. "Dreamtime" is an important part of Australian aboriginal life. Native Americans see dreams as special messages from the world of spirit.

Gypsies and Dreaming

Gypsies hold much stock in dreams and are renowned dream interpreters. Although Tunisian and Algerian Romanies are the recognized experts in this field, English Gypsies certainly have been practicing dream interpretation for many generations.

In common with all Gypsies, the English Travelers maintain that through dreams they are being given secret knowledge that could affect their future, positively or negatively. They believe dreams come from the spirits of their ancestors.

In my two earlier books on the Romani (*Secrets of Gypsy Fortunetelling* and *Secrets of Gypsy Love Magick*), I related how people would visit the Gypsies at their encampments, either to have their fortunes told or to learn about performing magic. Dream interpretation was, and still is, yet another reason for these visits. Many people—country born or city bred, it doesn't seem to matter which—are curious about the "nighttime movies of the mind" and wonder if these are perhaps something more than "movies" for the entertainment of their unconscious selves.

That there is a special significance to the act of dreaming has been determined by researchers. Dreams are indicated in a sleeping person by Rapid Eye Movement (REM). Researchers have found that if they awaken a subject as soon as he or she starts dreaming (starts REM), it will take a much shorter length of time to begin REM when the subject goes back to sleep. Awakened again, it will take a shorter time still to begin REM on returning to sleep, and so on. In fact, it seems to be the act of dreaming that is needed rather than the sleep itself. To take this to its extreme, it seems that a person who is not allowed to dream at all in sleep will then start to dream in the awakened state.

Gypsies are actually very observant and, in some ways, very prosaic. The first thing a knowledgeable Romani will do when asked about the significance of a particular dream is to inquire about the person's general health and eating habits. Most of us, Gypsies included, are aware that a lot of dreaming is simply the result of excesses in eating and/or drinking. Charles Bowness, in *Romany Magic* (Samuel Weiser, New York 1973) says:

> Apart from those dreams brought on by stomachic derangement there are also those occasioned by some bodily excitation due to a previous pleasant or unpleasant experience. Another cause is tension owing to brooding over some problem or fear of a future event.
>
> To categorize further, dreams of terror can be due to a slight and temporary disorder of the heart. Similarly, a defect in the lungs can be responsible for a dream of bloodshed. To experience some enormous difficulty in a dream, such as hacking a way through a jungle, or trying to penetrate a wall indicates disorder of the liver. Dreaming of sharp pains, knife stabs in the back and the like, is because of kidney disorder. If a dream contains some element of hypnotic regularity such as the swinging of a pendulum, then there may well be a tendency to anaemia.

It is obvious that one cannot simply take any dream and say, "Oh, yes. That means such-and-such." The question is, then, which dreams can be interpreted? The Gypsies say any dream that is especially vivid; one that stays with you after you wake. Additionally, it should be one that is dreamed when you are in good health and have not overindulged the night before.

Elaborating on the Dream

An immediate problem is that the unconscious mind does not like to let go. It does not like to leave a dream all nicely cut and dried. Rather, it will embellish, and keep on embellishing. So the longer you spend trying to remember the details of a dream, the more details you will remember, or seem to remember. For this reason it is of prime importance to write down every single detail that you remember about a dream as soon as you wake up. If you stop for breakfast, or even just a quick cup of coffee, you will find yourself "remembering" other things about the dream. Yet there is no guarantee that these things really were in the dream!

As the day progresses, and you keep reflecting on the dream, you will seem to remember more and more about it; you will seem to be filling in the blanks. But these "remembrances" are far more likely to be embellishments that the unconscious mind is now adding to make the dream story more interesting!

Just how "sneaky" the unconscious mind can be is detailed by Charles Godfrey Leland (*Gypsy Sorcery and Fortune Telling*, 1891), relating a dream he had once when staying in Germany:

> I thought I was in my bed yet I did not know exactly where I was. I at once perceived the anomaly, and was in great distress to know whether I was awake or in a dream. I seemed to be an invalid. I realized, or knew, that in another bed near mine was a nurse or attendant. I begged her to tell me if I were dreaming, and to awake me if I were. She tried to persuade me that I was in my ordinary life, awake. I was not at all satisfied. I arose and went (out) into the street. There I met with two or three common men. I felt great hesitation in addressing them on such a singular subject, but

told them I was in distress because I feared that I was in a dream, and begged them to shake or squeeze my arm. I forget whether they complied, but I went on and met three gentlemen, to whom I made the same request. One at once promptly declared that he remembered me, saying that we had met before in Cincinnati. He pressed my arm, but it had no effect. I began to believe that I was really awake. I returned to the room. I heard a child speaking or murmuring by the nurse. I asked her again to shake my hand. This she did so forcibly that I was now perfectly convinced that it was no dream. And the instant it came home to me that it was a reality, there seized me the thrill or feeling of a coming nightmare—and I awoke!

So the moment he determined that in fact he was not dreaming, he woke up . . . proving that, in fact, he was dreaming! Many times we have dreams where we are not sure whether we are dreaming or are actually awake. Sometimes you might seem to be awake, get up out of bed, get dressed, go out to the kitchen . . . and then, suddenly, find that you are still lying in bed! This is known as the "false awakening." In such an example, you have, in all probability, actually experienced a brief moment of astral projection, which ties in with many dreams (see Chapter 7 for more on astral projection).

Lucid Dreaming

On the opposite side, there are times when you can be dreaming and fully realize that you are asleep and dreaming. You can, in effect, watch your dream—much as a third party—and even direct it. This is known as "lucid dreaming" and I'll talk more about it later in this book.

To most people it is the mystery of the meaning of dreams that intrigues. When you do awaken, and when you remember what you have dreamed, then you want to know what that dream meant. Presuming that you have met the Gypsies' criteria—healthy, with no late evening over-indulgences—then we can examine what you experienced. The interpretations I present in this book are those that I have collected from Gypsies throughout the British Isles. I have studied many "dream dictionaries" and it seems to me that, for whatever reason, the Gypsies' interpretations are far more relevant than others'. Perhaps it's

Chapter 2

Symbolism
in Dreams

M odern science says that we spend between 25 percent and 50 percent of our sleeping time in the dream state. We have an average of six dream periods every night and each dream lasts anywhere up to forty minutes. Apparently if we didn't have these dreams we would go crazy. Most of them are from our unconscious mind, trying to get a message across to us for our own well-being.

Gypsies believe that these messages come from ancestral spirits. Who is to say they are wrong? That may be exactly what our unconscious mind is—proddings from the spirits. The point is that if we are being given these messages for our own well-being, it would behoove us to try to understand them, to listen to the spirits. The unconscious, or the spirits, employ symbols with which we are familiar. They present the message using objects that pertain to our everyday life, the better that we may understand what is being communicated.

Sigmund Freud believed that the unconscious mind contains repressed material—wishes, thoughts, experiences—that the individual will not accept into the conscious mind. These things are therefore repressed and often disguised. Carl Jung called this repressed material the "Personal Unconscious." He believed that there was also the "Collective Unconscious," which contained elements from racial memories and experiences.

Universal and Personal Symbolism

There are two kinds of symbols that come through to us in our dreams: *universal* symbols and *personal* symbols.

Suppose you dream about a castle. Now it could well be that you watch a lot of late night television and see many old movies featuring vampires, ghosts, or ogres of one sort or another living in castles. From this it could be that you automatically associate castles with evil. You might do this consciously or it might be an unconscious association. Either way when you think, see, or dream castles, you conceptualize "evil." Yet you could have a close friend who is interested in architecture and considers the castle to be a thing of beauty; the height of the architect's craft. For him or her the association of castles with evil is ridiculous. A third person might have grown up in Europe and actually have lived in a castle for a time. He or she considers them neither evil nor beautiful but simply cold, damp, and drafty!

So here there are three totally different reactions to castles. These, then, are *personal* interpretations. Any one of these three people having a dream about a castle would have to consider this personal association when deciding what the dream meant for them.

Yet there is also a *universal* symbolism for castles. They are associated with ambition. Ambition is one of the interpretations that would be used by the majority of people when they have no particularly strong, personal feelings about castles. As I say in *Buckland's Complete Book of Witchcraft* (Llewellyn, 1986):

> Universal Symbolism includes those things that remain true for all humankind throughout the ages. Included are colors, numbers, form, and sexual identity (i.e., male and female). They come from the super-consciousness and therefore are timeless.

I go on to give the example of transportation:

> (It is) the universal symbol of spiritual advancement. As material technology has advanced, the application of symbology has kept pace. So transportation may take one of the modern forms of conveyance, such as rockets, planes, steamships, trains, or automobiles, or one of the

timeless modes of riding on the back of an animal or walking.

When you set out to interpret your dreams, therefore, you need to look at each and every one of the symbols and decide what it means to *you*. If something has a special, *personal* meaning, then go with that. But if it has no special meaning, interpret according to the universal symbolism.

It stands to reason, therefore, that in the unlikely event of two people having identical dreams, they would not mean the same thing for both people. Just as in a card reading, no two cards mean exactly the same thing for two different people.

When a Gypsy interprets your dream, he or she will ask a lot of questions in order to find out the personal significance of each and every symbol.

In the listing of dream symbols in the Gypsy Dream Dictionary (Chapter 8), I can, of course, give only the universal meanings. What you have to do is to see whether or not that meaning fits for you or whether you have a stronger, more personal feeling with regard to that symbol; a feeling or interpretation that is far more significant to you as an individual. As Carl Jung said: "No dream symbol can be separated from the individual who dreams it."

Before we actually get to the listing of symbols and their universal meanings, I would like to further discuss interpretation and also talk about the prophetic dream—that which tells you something about the future. I'd also like to talk about how you can decide, ahead of time, what you *want* to dream . . . even if it's the winner of tomorrow's horse race!

Chapter 3

Dream Interpretation

In order to read the true meaning of your dreams, you must study the component parts and how they relate to one another. You can't just consider one thing and ignore everything else. By the same token, not *everything* in your dream is significant.

For instance, if you dream you enter a room and, on looking around, you see everything in the room—chairs, a table, bookcase, pictures on the wall, furnishings, decorations—not every single item has deep inner meaning and needs to be interpreted. Much of it is like the set dressing for a play or a movie; it is simply there to give a broad picture to frame the important and relevant action. This is the problem with many dream books that give explanations of 1,000, 10,000, 50,000 or however many dream symbols! You can get so wrapped up in checking everything you remember that you lose the main message of the dream. All you need check are the *major* components. These are the ones that really strike you; those that really stand out. Unless a picture on the wall of a room in your dream really catches your eye, you can ignore it as simple set decoration. On the other hand, if you find your eye being drawn strongly to that particular picture, or table, or whatever, then yes, that may well be of significance and is worth investigating.

Dream People

You should especially study the people in your dreams and how they relate to you. Generally the *main character* in a dream, whoever it happens to be, represents *you*. Let's say that you dream of your Uncle Charlie (someone you always liked and admired) and see him doing something he shouldn't be doing. For example, let's say he is drinking whiskey and smoking cigarettes; something he wouldn't normally do. The reason he's doing those things is that the "Uncle Charlie" in the dream is not your Uncle Charlie at all . . . it's *you!*

Your unconscious mind knows that to show yourself drinking and smoking would have little effect on you, since it is something you may do on a regular basis. But to show your favorite uncle drinking and smoking, when he doesn't normally do so, will have a strong impact on you. Perhaps it will make you break these habits, which your unconscious knows are not good for you.

As another example, you might dream that your little sister is using a long rawhide whip, whipping people standing around her! This doesn't make sense to you since your sister is a mild little thing, full of love for everyone. But the universal symbolism of a whip is a sharp tongue and bad temper—something that can really hurt people. In the dream, your sister represents yourself, again to make a bigger impact on you. Your unconscious mind is pointing out to you that your bad temper and sharp tongue can hurt others, and you should do something about it.

So the first thing to remember in interpreting your dreams is that not everyone is who they seem to be. So far as the main characters in the dream are concerned, they (one *or more* of them) just might be representing you. Look at the dream from that possibility first, to see if it makes sense. Study it to see if there are any other clues to the fact that it is you who is being shown there.

Interpreting the "Ordinary" Dream

Let's now look at a longer, more complicated dream in which you were shown as yourself. Suppose you were able to remember all, or most, of the details of a dream that seemed an ordinary one: a walk in the country.

You are walking along a country road with a knapsack on your back. The road is long and straight. Ahead of you is a crossroads. As you approach it, you hear the sound of castanets and, in the distance, a foghorn. An old, brown, farm wagon rumbles past you. In the back of the wagon sits a large cat. In the distance, across the fields, you can see a great forest. So, does all this mean anything?

Start out by examining the dream for any personal symbolism. Suppose you have a particularly strong association with cats. You always had a cat or kitten as a child and really love them. To you they represent love and affection. Therefore you should focus on this *personal* interpretation for the cat, rather than the universal symbolism interpretation given in the dictionary.

Now list the main points of the dream. They are as follows, together with their given meanings:

Knapsack: Need to get away and be alone.

Road: Things come easily to you.

Crossroads: A decision.

Castanets: Minor irritations.

Foghorn: Troubled times coming.

Wagon: Separation from loved ones.

Cat: Love and affection (*personal symbolism*).

Forest: Peace and tranquillity.

In interpreting your dream we can say that, until now, things have come fairly easily for you (*long, straight road*) but that there are now some minor irritations (*castanets*) entering the picture. These could develop into troubled times for you (*foghorn*). You need to get away and be by yourself for a while (*knapsack*), even though this will mean separating yourself from your loved ones *(wagon)*. You need to get down to the roots of your problem (the wagon was brown). Despite all this, peace and tranquility are obtainable *(forest in the distance)*.

Okay, but where does the cat come into it, you may ask? Well, it is riding in the wagon, which itself represents separation from loved ones. Since the cat symbolizes love and affection, we can say that, by extension, the cat is there as a representation of your loved one(s) being carried away from you by the wagon.

So, to simplify your dream, you have had a nice smooth time up until now, but there are troubles ahead. To get over them, you need to track them down to their roots. You need time alone to do this. But don't despair, you will come through it all okay.

You can see, then, that what seemed like a nice ordinary dream is, in reality, a warning of things to come. Why else would you have the dream unless it was to tell you something? You'll find that, similarly, there is a reason for all dreams. They are not simply "nighttime movies" for your entertainment!

Chapter 4

Lucid Dreaming

I have spoken of situations in which you realize that you are dreaming *during a dream*. This is known as *lucid* dreaming. It is not uncommon and can vary from a simple thought of "This is only a dream," to a feeling of incredible freedom from all restrictions and the seeming ability to do whatever you want. Usually, in lucid dreaming, you feel certain that you are awake and then you suddenly get some kind of clue in the dream that in fact you are not awake.

For example, a Gypsy I spoke with in Nottingham, England, told me of waking one morning and, believing that he was wide awake, getting up out of bed and getting dressed. He and his wife then went out to their car. As they got into the car he noticed that there was a wide river running past the back of his house . . . yet he knew there was no river within miles of where he lived! He said to his wife, "Look at that river. That must mean I'm dreaming." She replied that he was being ridiculous. She couldn't explain the river, but said that they had to be wide awake. In true Romani fashion, he was determined to prove that he was dreaming. He started the car, swung around the house and drove straight into the river! As the car hit the water he woke up, still in bed.

When you experience something like this—a realization that you are dreaming—you can sometimes go ahead and *direct* your dream. You can determine what it is you want to dream. But you must remain constantly alert. You need to keep reminding yourself that you are dreaming and, therefore, that you can do anything you like. Otherwise you will slip off back into the unconscious dream state and lose control.

Many dreamers enter this lucid area by way of nightmares. You might have a bad nightmare, something that is really frightening. You suddenly say to yourself in the dream, "This is ridiculous! This is only a dream. I don't need to be afraid!" When most people do this, either they wake up or else the nightmare retreats into a normal, non-frightening dream. But what you should do at this point is to *direct* the dream. Take yourself away from the nightmare aspect and move yourself on to something that you would enjoy. Incidentally, dream researchers have found that lucid dreams are more easily experienced in the morning hours just prior to waking. This half-asleep/half-awake condition is termed the *hypnapompic* state (when falling asleep at night, the term is *hypnagogic*).

In *A Study of Dreams* (1913)[1] Frederik van Eeden, a Dutch psychotherapist, says:

> I dreamt that I stood at a table before a window. On the table were different objects. I

---

1. *Proceedings of the Society for Psychical Research: XXVI*

was perfectly well aware that I was dreaming and I considered what sorts of experiments I could make. I began by trying to break glass, by beating it with a stone. I put a small tablet of glass on two stones and struck it with another stone. Yet it would not break. Then I took a fine claret-glass from the table and struck it with my fist, with all my might, at the same time reflecting how dangerous it would be to do this in waking life; yet the glass remained whole. But lo! When I looked at it again after some time, it was broken. It broke all right, but a little too late, like an actor who misses his cue. This gave me a very curious impression of being in a fake world, cleverly imitated, but with small failures.

I took the broken glass and threw it out of the window, in order to observe whether I could hear the tinkling. I heard a noise all right and I even saw two dogs run away from it quite naturally. I thought what a good imitation this comedy-world was. Then I saw a decanter with claret and tasted it, and noted with perfect clearness of mind: "Well, we can also have voluntary impressions of taste in this dream world; this has quite the taste of wine."

Many people who experience lucid dreaming report that such dreams are very easily remembered on awakening—much more so than any other dreams.

One of the fun aspects of lucid dreaming is to be able to meet with friends at a predetermined place in your dreams. In fact, there are various study groups around the country who "meet" on a regular basis as part of their exercises in dream investigation.

In *Astral Projection* (University Books, 1962), Oliver Fox relates how he and two friends, Elkington and Slade, once spent an enjoyable evening together discussing dreams and then agreed to meet on Southampton Common in England in their dreams that night. Fox himself had no trouble going to the Common in his dream, and became aware of meeting Elkington there. In the dream, both he and Elkington commented on the fact that Slade had not shown up.

The following morning Fox met with both men. Elkington reported the same dream that Fox had experienced. But Slade complained that he considered the experiment a failure; he hadn't dreamed at all. This explained why Fox and Elkington had not encountered him on the Common.

Chapter 5

Prophetic Dreams

When our ordinary waking consciousness or *will* goes to sleep or rest, or even dozes, at that instant an entirely different power takes command of the myriad forces of memory, and proceeds to make them act, wheel, evolute, and perform dramatic tricks, such as the common sense of our daily life would never admit."

So said Charles Godfrey Leland in 1891.[1] He went on to say:

> This power we call the dream, but it is more than that. It can do more than make *Us,* or *Me,* or the Waking Will, believe that we are passing through fantastic scenes. It can remember or revive the memory of things forgotten by *us*; it can, when *he* is making no effort, solve for the geometrician problems which are far beyond his waking capacity—it sometimes teaches the musician airs such as he could not compose. That is to say, within ourself (*sic*) there dwells a more mysterious Me, in some respects a more gifted Self. There is not the least reason, in the present state of Science, to assume that this is either a "spiritual" being or an act of material forces . . . This power, therefore, knows things hidden from Me, and can do what *I* cannot. Let no one incautiously exclaim here that what this really means is, that I possess higher accomplishments which I do not use. The power often

---

1. *Gypsy Sorcery and Fortune Telling,* Fisher-Unwin, London, 1891

actually acts against Me—it plays at fast and loose with me—it tries to deceive me, and when it finds that in dreams I have detected a blunder in the plot of the play which it is spinning, it brings the whole abruptly to an end with the convulsion of a nightmare, or by letting the *curtain* fall with a crash, and—I am awake! . . . With what wonderful speed all is washed away clean from the blackboard! Our waking visions do not fly like this. But—be it noted, for it is positively true—the evanescence of our dream is, in a vast majority of instances, exactly in proportion to their folly.

"This power, therefore, knows things hidden from me," Leland says. It certainly seems to. In many cases they are things that are not literally *unknown* to us, but simply "hidden." Yet there have been a number of recorded cases where things revealed to a dreamer very definitely *were* totally unknown.

The first part of the Koran, the holy scripture of Islam, was received by the Prophet Muhammad in a dream. In another dream, the faithful were promised possession of the holy city of Mecca. Not surprisingly, Muhammad attached great importance to dreams.

Before Waterloo, Napoleon dreamed of his coming defeat. Adolf Hitler, when a corporal of the Bavarian Infantry in World War One, had a dream that saved his life and, he felt, foretold that he would have a great destiny. Many famous inventors, most notably Thomas A. Edison, arrived at their inventions by way of dreams.

An early example of the prophetic dream is the case of an old tinker named John Chapman. Other than the fact that he was not nomadic, Chapman's lifestyle was pretty much like that of a Gypsy. He was a tinker/peddler living in the village of Swaffham, England, in the county of Norfolk, in the fifteenth century. He scraped a living mending pots and pans and selling odds and ends.

One night John Chapman had a strange dream. He dreamed that he was told to go to London and stand on London Bridge, where he would meet with a certain man who would bring him news of a fortune that he could have. When John told his neighbors of the dream, they laughed at him. But he was very moved by it. He felt he should go, though it was over a hundred miles to London and he had no horse to take him there. His neighbors told him to forget the dream but he decided otherwise. Chapman set out for London on foot.

In those days, London Bridge was a crowded, bustling span across the Thames River. The whole bridge was covered with buildings: houses and shops. When he finally arrived there, John Chapman stood in the middle of the bridge and waited. Nothing happened.

He waited there for three days, but no man appeared to him. He was loathe to go back home knowing he would be a laughingstock. On the morning of the fourth day a shopkeeper, opposite whose shop Chapman stood, went up to him and asked what he was waiting for. Chapman told him the story, though he did not give his name nor say from where he came. The shopkeeper heard him out, then laughed uproariously.

"You're a fool!" he cried. "Why, I had a strange dream myself a few nights ago, but I didn't go chasing across the country because of it." Chapman asked what the dream was about.

"Well," said the shopkeeper, "I dreamed of a little village in Norfolk called Swaffham, and of a man who dwelt there named John Chapman. In the dream he was a peddler and he had a pear tree in his back garden. Beneath this tree was buried a great store of treasure. Now, suppose I had gone all the way to Norfolk to dig under that tree? What a fool I'd be!" He laughed louder and louder, then returned to his store.

John Chapman lost no time in returning home. He made straight for the old pear tree in his back garden and dug down between its roots. There he found a vast fortune in gold and silver. In gratitude, Chapman gave a great deal of money to the village church. In fact, today you can go to the church in Swaffham, Norfolk, and see a wooden carving of the peddler on one of the pews, along with many stained glass windows depicting the story of his dream.

Such stories are not as uncommon as you might think. Many people in their dreams learn things of which they had no previous knowledge whatsoever. Another famous example is the case of Maria Marten.

In 1827, Maria Marten, daughter of a couple living in Suffolk County, England, ran away with her lover William Corder, a young farmer. The parents heard nothing from Maria for a long time, but finally got a letter from

Corder saying that their daughter was fine and that he and Maria had married. This set their minds at rest, though they never heard a word from Maria herself.

One night, about a year after Corder's letter, Maria's mother had a dream. In it she saw Corder murder Maria and hide her body under the floor of a large red barn. The dream was so vivid that the Martens journeyed to the Corder farm and there Mr. Marten tore up the floorboards of the barn. The rotting body of Maria was found buried in a sack. William Corder was charged with her murder, confessed, and finally was hanged for it.

A more recent example occurred again in Britain, this time in Wales in the little Welsh village of Aberfan, on the night of October 20, 1966. A little girl named Eryl Jones, nine years old, had a dream that there was no school the following day. Not just that there were no classes held, but that the school itself had disappeared. She told her mother the next morning that "something black came down all over it." But Eryl went off to school anyway.

Shortly after nine o'clock that morning, a half-million-ton mountain of coal waste, saturated by days of unrelenting rain, slid down over the village burying houses and the entire school. Nearly 150 people—most of them school-children—died, Eryl Jones among them.

Many other people in Britain had similar dreams of this coming disaster. In Plymouth, on England's south coast, a psychic "saw" the avalanche of coal slag pour down the mountainside onto the village. She saw many details, later verified, of the ensuing rescue attempts. One man who had never heard of the town dreamed of the word "Aberfan." Any number had the connection of coal and Wales. There were so many reports of detailed dreams prior to the tragedy that a survey was conducted. At least thirty-six prophetic dreams could definitely be confirmed. As a direct result of this, the British Premonitions Bureau and the (New York) Central Premonitions Registry were established.

Chapter 6

Dreaming for Profit

Is it possible to profit from one's dreams? I have already mentioned inventors who came by their inventions through the dream state. Writers and artists have also profited in this way. Charles Dickens freely admitted that he built many of his intriguing characters and detailed plots while sound asleep at night. Mary Shelley dreamed the entire story of Frankenstein. But there are more immediate ways that any one of us can actually profit through our dreams. One way is to dream the winner of a horse race.

Over twenty years ago, in 1978, a report came in to a British police station that a section of the main A-1 Highway had been blocked off. Rushing out to investigate, the "bobbies" found that a group of Gypsies was responsible.

There had been an argument between two Romani men over the merits of their respective horses. Finally the men had decided to race one another to see whose horse was faster. What better place to race, they thought, than down the main highway? So, with their vardos they blocked off a seven mile stretch and had their race! A Nottingham newspaper reported the event as follows:

GYPSIES SEAL OFF PART OF A-1 FOR DAWN HORSE RACE

Police in Nottinghamshire are looking into complaints that Gypsies shut off seven miles of the great North Road with their vehicles and turned it into a racecourse.

Villagers alongside the A-1 between Sutton-on-Trent and Tuxford said yesterday that 250 Gypsies, some from as far away as Scotland, closed the road for twenty minutes while two Gypsy families decided which of them owned the best horse. One family was from Surrey and one from Doncaster. Each staked £2,000 on the race along the A-1. Side bets totaled several thousand pounds.

The race, run at 6:00 a.m. on Sunday last week, was won by the northern horse, which completed the course in nineteen minutes. After the race the winning owner rejected an offer of £3,500 for it.

Police in the nearby town of Retford said: "We did not know it was happening and we are looking into it. No one has the right to close a trunk road, certainly not for horse racing." But inquiries were difficult because the Gypsies left the district after the race.

The horse, not the dog, is considered by the Romani to be "man's best friend." Gypsy horse dealers are the most knowledgeable anywhere in the world. Being so appreciative of horses, Gypsies—men and women—very much enjoy horse racing and, with their knowledge, usually do very well betting on the races.

Some Gypsies in Kent told me of a man (a *gaujo,* or non-Gypsy) they used to know who *dreamed* of horse race winners. I did some research and found that this appears to be true. The man lived in London and his name was Harold Horwood. He was an electrical engineer and his wins had been documented and verified by the London newspaper the *Sunday Pictorial.* Horwood consistently won a great deal of money over a period of several years, placing bets according to his dreams.

He said that on one occasion "the name of the winner was shouted at me (in the dream) so loudly that it woke me up!" The exciting thing about this is that Horwood claimed that anyone can learn his technique. Indeed, in later years, his wife also started dreaming winners. Several of the Gypsies to whom I spoke with tried it and they too had success.

For many years Horwood had been interested in spirit communication then later developed an interest in prophetic dreams. After a couple of tentative tries, he woke up one morning in 1945 with a word that sounded like "Sehoney" ringing in his ears. The Cambridgeshire race was soon to be run and in looking through the list of runners, Horwood saw a horse named *Sayani.* Since the name was so similar, he backed it for a modest five pounds. He received £200 when it won.

Inspired by this, he concentrated on the Manchester November Handicap race, and dreamed of the flashing letters "L. V. G." Looking at the runners, he backed *Las Vegas* with forty pounds and walked away with £800. There were twenty-three runners in that race and the horse won at odds of 20:1. So in just two races, Horwood won £1,000 (a U.S. equivalency of about $2,500 at that time).

Symbolism often came into discovering the winners. In April of 1947, Horwood dreamed about a pride of lions playing together, with one lioness amongst them. The next day, *Lion Lass* won a race. On the eve of the 1948 Cesarwitch race, he dreamed he was on the deck of a ship when a log of wood burst into bright flame. He stamped it out, but it burst alight a second time. Again he stamped it out, but once more it happened, and he kept putting out the flaming log for the rest of the night! The next day he had some hesitation when he found one horse racing named *Woodburn* and another named *Sea Smoke*. However, he didn't remember noticing any smoke in the dream so he bet on Woodburn. He won at 100:9.

A dream of "Mallory Marshes" translated to *Marshmallow*, another winner. Just before the 1949 Derby, he remembered dreaming of a six-letter word with two syllables. He couldn't recall the word exactly, but he knew it was a not-too-uncommon word. *Nimbus* won at 7:1. The only other names with six letters and two syllables were *Tangui* and *Xermes*—decidedly unusual names. For the 1952 Derby he got the name clearly: *Tulyar*. It won at 11:2. And so it went on, year after year.

The Society for Psychical Research learned of Horwood's precognition and examined the records. They claimed that they were "far and away the best we have received in this direction" (June 9, 1958). The Society referred him to a "team" of dreamers, the members of which all concentrated on one particular race, then sent a record of their dreams to the team captain for interpretation. In this way it was possible to really pinpoint a horse. However, after a time of working with the team, Horwood came to the conclusion that the best person to interpret a dream is the dreamer him or herself (due to the personal symbolism I have mentioned) and returned to working alone.

Horwood's account of the 1958 Ascot Stakes is also interesting:

> Concentrated on this race. Dreamed that *Secretary* would win. This was subsequently amplified by a statement (in my dream) that the winner was the secretary to the manager or owner or someone like that. Of the horses running there were none named *Secretary,* but *Sandiacre* was the only horse beginning with "S." It also had the same number of letters as "Secretary." I backed it and it won at 100:7. A very interesting and instructive thing occurred the following morning when reading the story of the race. The *Daily Mail* had printed, in half-inch type, "Sandiacre was willed to win," and made a prominent point of the fact that Mary Dutton, the *secretary* of the trainer, had willed the horse to win by running with it and cheering it until it passed the post.

There seems to be no consistency in the manner in which the winners are indicated in dreams. Horwood's wife had a dream prior to The Oaks in June 1958. She told her husband how she had dreamed that a ball got into her room, but every time she tried to throw it out, it would not leave her hand. She said to her husband, "If only there *was* a horse named *Tantalizer*—the dream was so tantalizing." He checked and found that there was a horse named Tantalizer running in The Oaks. He bet on it. It lost! The race was won by *Bella Paola*. Horwood later said, "This shows you should stick to strict interpretation of the dream, not what someone says about the dream." The ball was Bella; Horwood's wife's name was Pauline . . . *Bella Paola*.

On the morning of the Fenwolf Stakes that same year, Horwood woke up with the words "can't tell you" on his lips. He didn't know why and couldn't remember any dream, but on checking the runners, he found *Cantelo*. He backed it and it won at 7:4. Examples go on over many years. Sometimes the name itself is dreamed or a close approximation; sometimes the initial(s), sometimes a number relating to the number of letters in the name, and sometimes it is purely symbolic.

Another way of finding the winner, says Horwood, is over a period of time by a process of elimination. Start by putting all the names in boxes. For example, suppose there are sixteen names. It will require four dreams to narrow down the winner. Let's call the horses Jack, Tom, Dick, Harry, Paul, John, Jim, Sam, Ann, Gertrude, Fanny, Ethel, May, Fay, Babe, and Lil. The first day put half in one box and half in another:

Left Box	Right Box
Jack	Ann
Tom	Gertrude
Dick	Fanny
Harry	Ethel
Paul	May
John	Fay
Jim	Babe
Sam	Lil

Have that list beside your bed when you go to sleep. Tell yourself that you will dream of the winner.

The next day, rearrange the names so that the first and last four go in the left box and the second and third four go in the right box:

Left Box	Right Box
Jack	Paul
Tom	John
Dick	Jim

Harry	Sam
May	Ann
Fay	Gertrude
Babe	Fanny
Lil	Ethel

Again, go to sleep with this on the bedside table and the thought that you will dream of the winner.

For the third night, make out the list with alternate pairs, left and right:

Left Box	**Right Box**
Jack	Dick
Tom	Harry
Paul	Jim
John	Sam
Ann	Fanny
Gertrude	Ethel
May	Babe
Fay	Lil

For the fourth and final night, put them alternately in the boxes:

Left Box	Right Box
Jack	Tom
Dick	Harry
Paul	John
Jim	Sam
Ann	Gertrude
Fanny	Ethel
May	Fay
Babe	Lil

Here is a review of these listings, perhaps making them easier to understand:

Horse	Number	1st List	2nd List	3rd List	4th List
Jack	1	L	L	L	L
Tom	2	L	L	L	R
Dick	3	L	L	R	L
Harry	4	L	L	R	R
Paul	5	L	R	L	L
John	6	L	R	L	R
Jim	7	L	R	R	L
Sam	8	L	R	R	R
Ann	9	R	R	L	L

Gertrude	10	R	R	L	R
Fanny	11	R	R	R	L
Ethel	12	R	R	R	R
May	13	R	L	L	L
Fay	14	R	L	L	R
Babe	15	R	L	R	L
Lil	16	R	L	R	R

Now, if as a result of analyzing your dreams over the four days, you find that the first day gave you "left," the second "left," the third "right," and the fourth "left," then the only horse that corresponds to that pattern is Dick, as can be seen in the previous table. This horse might also be underscored by other indications in the dream.

Anther method, that doesn't necessarily call for a lot of dreams over several nights, is to put the names into a number of boxes before you go to sleep at night:

Left Row	**Right Row**
Jack	Tom
Dick	Harry
Paul	John
Jim	Sam

Ann	Gertrude
Fanny	Ethel
May	Fay
Babe	Lil

Horwood used this method quite a lot. For example, he might dream of filling his car with gas and seeing the needle of the gas gauge point to the top right, while the attendant said, "Hurry up. Hurry up." This would indicate the top right box and the name *Harry*. Another time, using this method, Horwood saw a young woman come out of a room into a passageway with doors on either side. The door she emerged from was the first on the left, and she carried a baby in her arms. This obviously indicates the horse *Babe* in the bottom left box.

Whichever method you use, says Horwood, two things are essential. One is to tell your unconscious mind, emphatically, just before you go to sleep, that you *will* dream of the winner. The other is to have pencil and paper beside the bed so that you can write down everything you remember *as soon as you wake up*. You should keep a flashlight there also, in case you wake up in the middle of the night. The Gypsies I originally spoke to about this also emphasized these two essentials. They said that Horwood's methods worked for them. They could work for you, too.

Summary

1. Start out with at least some degree of expectation that you will be successful. In other words, think positive.

2. Have a writing pad and pencil beside the bed, plus a small flashlight. I would even recommend sharpening the pencil at both ends and attaching it to the notebook with a piece of string, so you don't lose it as you grope for it.

3. Decide on a race about a week ahead of time. Start with races that have smaller fields (numbers of horse).

4. List the runners' names in any order, preferably haphazard, so that you aren't swayed by those at the top of the list. Number them one, two, three, etc., and make a left and a right column, as described earlier.

5. Keep the list at the side of the bed and read it all the way through several times before going to sleep. There's no need to try to memorize it. The Gypsies suggest reading it through seven times in all.

6. Say to yourself—out loud if you wish—at least three times, "I want to know which horse is going to win." If you are using the left/right column method over the four days, add: "I want to know whether it is in the left or the right column."

7. Write down all you can remember *as soon as you become conscious.* Don't expect to dream of a horse race; you seldom, if ever, do. You will get the name by clues, initials, numbers, symbols, etc.

8. Don't be discouraged if you don't remember your dreams. Keep trying. It can sometimes take weeks, months, or more, so don't be discouraged.

Chapter 7

Astral Projection

Many times, what you remember of your dreams is nothing but a confused mishmash of places and events. None of it seems to make any sense; no one part seems to be a logical continuance of the previous part. This is because you are actually remembering only the high points of a number of dreams, and one is running into another. For example, you might wake up with vague memories of drifting down the Nile River in a Chinese junk, which suddenly disappears and leaves you fighting the Confederate Army armed with nothing but a salmon fishing pole! What does this mean?

What it means is that you are remembering bits and pieces of more than one dream. Your first dream might have been of being on a fishing holiday in Scotland, fishing for salmon. Your next dream might have involved traveling down the Yangtze River in a sampan. Another dream might have been of the pyramids in Egypt, and a further dream might have been witnessing a battle of the Civil War. But bits and pieces of these dreams—odd high points of memory—were all that remained when you awoke, and they were all intermingled.

But there may be more to it than that. Perhaps you actually *did go* to Scotland, and Egypt, and the Far East! Not you physically, of course, but your ethereal body on the astral plane. The body as we know it has an invisible double known variously as the spirit, ethereal body, or astral double. It is an exact duplicate of its physical counterpart. Many believe, and research seems to bear it out, that in your dreams, this astral version of yourself actually does all the things you dream you are doing. You dream you climb Mount Everest? Your astral double actually does climb Mount Everest on the astral plane. You dream you have a date with a popular movie star? Your astral double has such a date with (the astral body of) the movie star. Interestingly enough, in the last example, if you were able to question said star, you may well find that he or she had memory of a dream that corresponds to yours (see the episode of Oliver Fox and his two friends in Chapter 4).

It is your astral body which stands in for you in your dreams. It is able to travel incredible distances in the blink of an eye. And, should an emergency arise—like the cat suddenly jumping on your chest as you sleep, or the smoke alarm sounding off—it is able to "snap" back into your body immediately. You may have had the experience of a sudden "jump" of your body that brings you wide awake. It is possible that that is the impact of your astral body returning suddenly for whatever reason.

It cannot be said with certainty that every single dream was an astral journey. However, it is possible and certainly indications are that most dreams are such.

The exciting thing about astral projection is that it's possible for just about everyone to learn how to do it consciously. In other words, to decide where you would like to travel on the astral plane (or in the dream state) and what you would like to experience, and then to go to sleep and follow the set program. Basically all it takes is practice . . . and a lot of patience!

The first step is to teach yourself to remember every detail of your dreams. Again, all it takes is practice and patience. Keep a notebook and pencil beside your bed and, *first thing on waking,* write down everything you remember of your dreams. When I say "first thing on waking," I mean just that. Don't get up out of bed. Don't dress. Don't have a cup of coffee. Any delay will result in loss of memory of the dreams or the distortion of them. As soon as yours eyes open, *immediately* grab that pencil and paper and start writing!

To start with, you may remember very little. Don't worry. Write down that small amount anyway. If you do this every morning, you'll soon find that you are remembering more and more. Not only more details of a dream, but more dreams. As I've said before, you have about a half dozen dreams each night. You'll soon be able to separate one from another and get all the details.

I know of a woman who is able to wake herself after each dream, and record the details. Then she lies down again and goes back to sleep for the next one!

The next step is to decide where you want to go or what experience you would like to have, before you go to sleep. In your "dream journal" (let's call your note-book that) note something like: "Will go to Boston and see where Paul Revere hung his lanterns in the Old North Church."

Then go to sleep keeping these directions firmly in your mind. If you are planning on going somewhere you have been before then, as you fall asleep, imagine yourself going over the route to get there. See yourself leaving your house, driving along the roads, noticing any landmarks. As usual, on waking, note the details of your dreams.

It may turn out that you went nowhere near Boston (or wherever). Don't be discouraged; just keep trying. Eventually you will be able to direct yourself where you will.

Using the previous example, suppose you did dream of going to Boston and visiting the sights. If you have never been to Boston in real life, then check on the details you noted from your dream the following day. The overall appearance of the Old North Church will be easily confirmed from photographs. Check photographs, reference books, or the Internet for the other smaller details in your dream journal. You will probably be surprised to find that they all check out. Although you have never been there before, you have seen and recorded details of the journey and the area. Here will be proof that your astral body really did make the journey.

You will by now notice that you are actually *living* the dream. Rather than a blank period of sleep followed by remembrance of the dreams, you will feel that you are actually there at the time, participating.

Let's go a step further. You now pretty much have control of yourself on the astral plane. At some point in your dream, stop yourself and decide to go back and look at your sleeping physical body. You will find yourself in your bedroom, standing beside the bed or floating up by the ceiling, looking down at an inert figure that looks exactly like you. That the room is in darkness does not matter; you will see everything perfectly. You will feel that the astral you is the real you and that the figure in the bed is just a shell. You may—though not everybody can—see a fine, silver thread connecting your astral body to your physical body. This is the "silver cord" mentioned by most astral travelers. The Gypsies, too, speak of it. It is infinitely elastic. Wherever you go, even to the other side of the world, the cord will stretch, connecting your physical body to your astral body. This is your lifeline and is responsible for pulling you back to your physical body in case of emergency. As I've mentioned, any sort of interruption, such as the alarm clock going off, will cause your immediate return no matter how far away you are. It is this silver cord which, at the moment of death, finally severs from the physical body, allowing your astral body, or spirit, to progress.

Some writers, especially in fiction, have made much of the fact that your silver cord can be cut by negative (evil) forces, making it impossible for you to return to your body! This is basically a needless fear and should not stop you from attempting astral projection. It is *extremely* unlikely that you would be so attacked. The only possibility I could see would be if you were heavily into black magic or

Satanism and were constantly dealing with such negative forces to the point where they were seeking you out. Even then it's highly unlikely that the cord could be severed. You see, the slightest threat to your physical body, or to the cord itself, would mean your *immediate* return to your body. It is just like the fuse found on kitchen and bathroom wall sockets (GFCIs or Ground Fault Circuit Interrupters, now mandatory in all bathrooms, garages, and outdoor wiring). The slightest hint of a problem and the fuse blows to protect the line before any damage can be done.

Another method of astral projection is the induced trance. This can be done at almost any time; you don't have to wait until you go to bed to astrally project. The trance is the hazy borderline between waking and sleeping, and with a little practice can be fairly readily attained. It helps to be well rested, so that you do not fall into a deep, natural sleep, and also to have recently eaten, so that your attention is not distracted by hunger spasms. Choose a time and place where you can be absolutely quiet and free of interruption. No radios or televisions heard dimly in the background, no traffic roaring past the outside of the house—no sound at all.

Lie in the most comfortable position, either on your back or on your side, on a couch or bed, and let your eyelids close. Relax and breathe deeply and evenly. Relaxation and deep, regular breathing are very important. Lie there and feel your entire body relaxing by degrees. Think to yourself: "My feet are relaxing; they are relaxing; they are completely at ease. All aches and tiredness has flowed away from them as they relax. My legs are relaxing; all the muscles of my legs are relaxing. They are warm and comfortable; completely relaxed; completely at rest. My thighs are relaxing . . . ." Continue with all the limbs, going through the whole body. Concentrate on each area and will it to relax: feet, legs, body, hands, arms, neck, head. Breathe deeply and regularly all the time.

When the entire body has been covered, and you are completely at ease, with your eyes closed, start to think of your surroundings: the couch or bed on which you are lying, the rug, the curtains on the window, the other furniture in the room.

The first few times you try astral projection, you may have little success. Eventually, however, you will find that you are able to "see" the room around you even with your eyes closed. Just lie and imagine the room. Think of the positions of the furniture, the patterns of the wallpaper and upholstery. Suddenly you will realize that rather than imagining, you are actually seeing these things!

At this stage, or even slightly before, you may feel a strange sensation; a numbness that starts at your feet and gradually moves up through your whole body. This sensation is actually the separating of your astral body from your physical body. You will have absolutely no desire whatsoever to move. You may think to yourself that if you really wanted to, you could lift an arm or move a leg, but you just can't be bothered! All that is necessary now is to will yourself to leave your body, and you will drift out of it. You will be able to stand up beside your recumbent physical body.

It sometimes happens that as you lie, relaxing and breathing deeply, you get a sudden feeling that your eyes are rolling upward. It is as though you are looking up and back into your own brain, toward the pineal gland. You may then get a sensation of rushing upward toward the top of your head, until you suddenly find yourself standing beside yourself, calmly and at peace. This is known as

"Exiting by the Pineal Door," or "Pineal Door Projection." It does not often happen, but don't be surprised or afraid if it does.

Should you ever be in a state of partial release, don't worry. Partial release is when you feel your astral self is almost ready to leave the physical body, but not quite! You may lift your (astral) arms but feel that the rest of you is tied down. Just relax and tell yourself that if your arms are ready, then so is the rest of you. Sit up and then stand up. You will have no problem. Alternatively, think of yourself as sliding up into your head and out the Pineal Door, and it will happen.

Probably when you first leave your body you will experience dual consciousness. You will feel yourself in your astral body standing up, but at the same time you will feel yourself in your physical body lying down. Just concentrate on the "you" in the astral body and go on your way. The physical feeling will disappear.

Another excellent way of experiencing astral projection is via the "false awakening" mentioned earlier (see Chapter 1). Most people have had the experience of half waking in the morning and knowing, or being told, that it is time to get up out of bed and get dressed. They get out of bed and sleepily start to dress. They may ponder what to wear, reach a decision, then dress fully. Suddenly the alarm clock goes off again or someone calls and—surprise—they realize they are still lying in bed! Yet they would have sworn that they actually got up out of bed and got dressed. This was the astral body that acted out the arising. If you can realize at the time that it is the astral body acting out the morning ritual, then you can grasp that fact and carry on from there, remaining in the astral body. It is just recognizing the false awakening for what it is that is the difficult part. Often the shock of realization is enough to snap you right back into your body.

The only way you can gradually come to realize you are not really awake is to look out for falsities—things which, although they seem absolutely real, obviously could not be. You might "wake up" and, as you are getting dressed, notice a suit of armor standing in the corner of the room. You know that you do not own a suit of armor, yet the whole scene seems absolutely real. Concentrate, then, on making the armor disappear. It will eventually do so and that is your confirmation that you are on the astral plane.

On the astral plane, you can go virtually anywhere at the speed of thought. The astral plane itself can have the appearance of anything, as can you. It usually seems that you are in your normal everyday surroundings (because that's what you know best), and you look like yourself in appearance. But if you wished, you could change things. Think of yourself with red hair, and you have red hair. A mustache and beard? You have a mustache and beard. Think of yourself as being just that little bit taller you've always wanted to be, and you'll be taller! Think of yourself sitting in a restaurant halfway around the world, and you'll be there—instantly.

More from habit than anything you'll find yourself opening doors to go through them and pulling out chairs to sit down. But that's unnecessary. You can "think" yourself through doors and float on air. In other words, you can act like the proverbial ghost. In fact, what are taken to be ghosts are sometimes the astral forms of living people that have somehow become visible to an observer for a short period.

The doors, chairs, and other props you encounter on the astral are simply "astral props" to help you accommodate to the plane. As in the afterlife,[1] they are there because that is what you have come to expect. They are really unnecessary, but they are helpful. You can move these astral objects, but you cannot, in your astral body, move physical objects on the physical plane.

Generally, as an astral body you are invisible to others still in their physical bodies. I say "generally" because certain sensitives are able to focus in on astral beings.

There are many other ways of inducing astral projection, but the ones I have given above will do to start you on the path—and these are the safest ways for the beginner. Not everyone can have success. More correctly, not everyone will have memory of their success, for everyone does travel on the astral in their dreams. Don't forget to write down everything you remember, for in this way you will grow more proficient at attaining astral projection.

Do you still need dream interpretation for astral projection? Probably yes. When you become really proficient at projecting, then most of your "dreams" will be astral travels that you have planned, but there will still be a large

---

1. See my book *Doors To Other Worlds*, Llewellyn, 1996

number of pure dreams in there. Even when there are spontaneous projections that you afterward become aware of, these need to be interpreted. If it was an astral journey, *why* did you go to such a place and do such things as you remember? And if it was "just a dream," why did you go there and do that? For interpretation, see Chapter 3, and then turn to the Gypsy Dream Dictionary in Chapter 8 to sort out the details and find the meanings.

Conclusion

The world of dreams can be as fascinating as the world of Gypsies. Through your dreams you can learn more about yourself. You can learn of your past, present, and future. You can even dream to make a profit.

Dreaming, and dream interpretation, can be lots of fun, educational, and extremely enlightening . . . all at no cost to you! Happy dreams and *kushti bok*[2]!

—Raymond Buckland

---

2. Romanes for "Good luck!"

Chapter 8

Gypsy Dream Dictionary

I n this dictionary of dream symbols, I can, of course, only give the universal meaning. What you have to do is to see whether that meaning fits for you or whether you have a stronger, more personal feeling with regard to that symbol; a feeling or interpretation that is far more significant to you. As Carl Jung said: "No dream symbol can be separated from the individual who dreams it."

ABBEY/MONASTERY: Sanctuary; temporary safety. To dream that you are in an abbey is confirmation that you are safe and need not worry needlessly, though this safety may only be temporary. To come upon an abbey unexpectedly is a sign that there is help around the corner. Apply this to any worries you may have and look at the other symbols in the dream and how they relate to this.

ABBOT: Someone has a power or authority over you; they can make you do things you don't necessarily want to do. There is a restriction in your life. You may not be aware of this consciously, so examine your situation and those with whom you are in close contact.

ABORTION: You will not succeed in the project you are presently working on. Better make alternate plans.

ABYSS: Exercise caution for there is possible danger ahead. An abyss can also mean an invitation—to adventure, opportunity . . . or danger.

ACCEPTANCE: For some reason this seems to work with opposite meaning. Slow and laborious progress before final acceptance (in a dream) indicates quick success to come, while easy acceptance indicates trouble ahead. Acceptance can be shown in many ways. Perhaps, in your dream, you propose to a young lady and she accepts. An easy, almost immediate acceptance would forebode trouble ahead. Gypsies say that for a young woman to dream that she has accepted her lover's marriage proposal is a sign that there will be an unexpected delay in their wedding plans.

ACCIDENT: Any sort of an accident—car, household, job-related—is indicative of self-criticism. You have done something of which you are not proud. Examine your recent actions and see if you can undo the problem.

ACCORDIAN: A popular Gypsy instrument. To dream of playing an accordian indicates that you are having to work hard to achieve your desires. Yet if you dream that you are having a wonderful, happy time playing it, perhaps with lots of people dancing to the music, then it means you are enjoying your job and are happiest when working.

ACCUSATION: Torment; distress; self doubt. If, in your dream, someone points the finger at you, then it is really you doubting yourself.

ACE: To dream of playing cards, or handling cards, and especially noticing one of the aces, means that you will be a key figure in a love affair (ace of hearts), a law suit (ace of clubs), a legacy (ace of diamonds), or a scandal (ace of spades).

ACORN(S): The Gypsies say that dreaming of acorns means your plans will take a while to come to fruition, but when they do they will far exceed your greatest hopes.

ACTOR/ACTRESS: If you see yourself as an actor or actress, then you will be the bearer of good news. If you meet with, or watch (as part of an audience), actor(s) then you will be the recipient of good news.

ADDRESS: To write out an address on a letter indicates that you have found direction; you now know where you are going. You have set your goals and can move forward.

ADMIRAL: See Miltary Officer.

ADORATION: To be the object of adoration in a dream indicates that you can be a big flirt. You should beware of becoming conceited. If, in the dream, you are the one who is doing the adoring, beware of being misled; exercise caution.

AIRPLANE: In general, transportation symbolizes spiritual advancement. Examine the rest of the dream and see if it does, indeed, tie-in with that interpretation. If so, this modern, rapid form of transportation needs to be handled carefully lest it crash. If not, then it may simply indicate rapid advancement with opportunity for self-expression, especially if you are the pilot of the plane.

AISLE: A division; a parting. To dream of the aisle of a church often indicates a coming disagreement between two factions of a family. Gypsy families will always ensure that they are all together on one side of a church aisle, rather than some on one side and some on the other.

ALARM CLOCK: You are afraid of growing old. You have many plans and wonder if you'll ever have time to implement them all. See also Clock.

ALDER: An alder tree is an omen of happiness and coming good news. See also Tree.

ALLIGATOR: See Crocodile.

ALMS: To give or to receive alms indicates that your business will be successful and you will become wealthy.

ALTAR: Prosperity; peace. A center point; a focal point.

AMBULANCE: To see an ambulance indicates that you should exercise caution or you may have an accident. To be riding in an ambulance means you have made a grave error. Look back over your recent actions and see if you can spot the error and rectify it.

ANCHOR: Foundation; security. You have some base, some foundation upon which to build. You are secure. But it also should be kept in mind that an anchor can hold you back when you want to be moving.

ANGEL: Coming news that may or may not be good. It may well be that what, at first glance, appears to be good news is, on closer examination, bad news—and vice versa.

ANIMALS: See individual animal names.

ANTS: If you dream of ants on your clothing, or coming into your home, you will have petty annoyances. To watch ants is to indulge in activity; usually a lot of small jobs. An anthill is a sign of avoidance of work.

ANVIL: See Blacksmith.

APE/MONKEY: Symbolizes deceit. Beware of business associates trying to cheat you. Judge friends by their actions rather than by their words.

APPLE: An old Gypsy belief says that "Should a girl wish to dream of her future husband, it is necessary for her to obtain an apple from a widow on Saint Andrew's Eve. She must not give thanks for receipt of the apple, and should eat half of it before midnight, and the other half after midnight. Her future lover will then be revealed whilst she is asleep." See also Fruits.

APRICOTS: See Fruits.

APRON: To be wearing an apron means you will be taking orders from another, but getting satisfaction from it.

ARCHBISHOP: See Abbot.

ARCHERY: See Arrow.

ARM: If it is an arm offered to you, it can mean assistance. If you find an arm barring your way, exercise caution; carefully think through any plans you have for the future. A broken arm means the death of a relative (Gypsies say the left arm represents a female and the right arm a male). An arm that is excessively hairy indicates money coming to you.

ARMCHAIR: Whether the armchair is empty or whether you are sitting in it doesn't matter. It means that you are firmly established in your present position and no one can move you out of it without your permission.

ARMOR: To dream of being dressed in a suit of armor means you feel very secure, especially regarding financial matters. To see a suit of armor on display means you are worried about lack of security.

ARMY: Armed men are generally a good sign. If it is a marching army then great things are afoot, with many major forces at work, usually in your favor. A battle indicates a scandal.

ARREST: If you are arrested in your dreams it means you are taking unnecessary chances. Be more cautious.

ARROW: Usually a bad omen. An arrow shot by someone else and hitting you means there will be bad gossip about you. If you shoot an arrow in the air, your lover is unfaithful. See also Shooting.

ASHES: To dream of ashes in a stove, or fireplace, or to dream of clearing ashes, means you feel the work you are doing is beneath you. You are dissatisfied with your job.

ASS/DONKEY: A quarrel between friends. If it is trotting, it means disappointed hopes; if running, disaster. But to be given a donkey or an ass is a sign of business success. To be thrown off the back of one or to be kicked by one means a quarrel with your lover. If you hear an ass bray, it is great scandal. A heavily laden donkey indicates coming good fortune.

ASSASSIN: Relief from unpleasant circumstances. Final gratification.

ASYLUM/PSYCHIATRIC HOSPITAL: To be held in an asylum means you are not understood by your associates and have a hard time explaining yourself. To see others means you need to take great care in expressing yourself or you will be misunderstood. To see someone you know held there means you are worried about a friend. See also Madness.

AUCTION: To be at an auction means you will be getting an unexpected raise in pay. To be the auctioneer means you will have to work hard to earn the raise.

AUNT: See Uncle/Aunt.

AUTOMOBILE: Another symbol of spiritual advancement. Note the speed at which it is traveling . . . or is it standing still? If going up hill, obviously you are really having to work at your progress. A breakdown indicates that you need to reassess your beliefs and practices. See also Hot Rod.

AXE: To be wielding an axe means you are respected by others, though more for your position than for your abilities.

BABY/CHILD: To dream of a sleeping baby or small child means you have a shy, trusting nature. A baby crawling about means you will need to think quickly and make quick decisions. A crying child means you will have a number of small problems to resolve. To breastfeed a baby, or see a baby being breastfed, means you must beware of confiding in people who are not very close friends.

BACHELOR: A man dreaming that he is a bachelor should be cautious in his dealing with women. But according to an old Gypsy woman in Kent, when a woman dreams of a bachelor, it is an indication that her lover is fickle.

BACKDOOR: There is an unexpected solution to a problem you have. You should search for it; it may be well hidden, but it is there.

BACKPACK: See Knapsack.

BADGER: A badger is a sign of wisdom and sagacity (discerning).

BAGPIPES: To see and/or hear bagpipes being played means that help is coming to you from an unexpected source. Scottish Gypsies put great store in this dream symbol.

BAILIFF/SHERIFF: If you see a sheriff arrest someone, it means there will be arguing within your family. A sheriff coming to take your possessions means you will be facing a lawsuit, but that you will be successful in it. See also Police.

BAKER/BAKERY: Gain; increase. This could be financial gain or it could be increase in the size of your family— a child! It is more likely to be the latter if someone hands you a loaf of bread, say the Gypsies. Overall, anything to do with a bakery symbolizes joy. See also Eating/Drinking (Bread) and Meeting.

BALL: Something difficult to hold onto. If it is rolling away from you, then you must work harder to get ahead. If it is rolling towards you, then you can sit back and reap your just reward.

BALLOON: It seems solid but, in reality, it is just full of air! Don't be distracted by bright colors. Examine any personal or business offers you receive to make sure they are sound. A hot air balloon, however, whether you are ascending in one or just watching one go up, is always indicative of financial gain.

BALLROOM/DANCING: A ballroom filled with dancers indicates a happy family life. An empty ballroom shows a longing for company and/or family. Intricate dancing symbolizes an ability to do well in anything you try. To see others dancing means you will get pleasure from someone else's good fortune. To be dancing yourself means you will get pleasure from work that you do yourself.

BANDANA: For a woman to be wearing a bandana, or *diklo*, over her hair means she will soon be married. For an already-married woman to dream this means she will have a love affair.

BANJO: To see or hear a banjo being played indicates that you will have a good time socially.

BARBER/HAIRDRESSER: To be shaved by a barber is a bad omen. To have your hair cut means you should beware of gossip. To have your hair styled means you should pay more attention to your appearance.

BARE/NAKED: If you suddenly become naked, it means you will get a surprise, which could be good or bad. If you are the only person who is naked in a group, it is a warning of scandal to come. If all are naked, it is a sign of warmth, joy, and friendliness.

BARLEY: Good fortune.

BARN: The Gypsies say that to dream of a full barn means you will never go hungry again. But to dream of an empty barn indicates a life of sadness and want. A barn on fire indicates that you could lose all that you have.

BARREL: Similar to a barn, in that a full barrel indicates plenty and an empty one indicates want. If you are banging a stopper into a barrel then you need to secure what you have.

BARTENDER: If you are the bartender, then you will be mixing with company that is beneath you. If you are being served by a bartender, you should beware of any advice offered freely to you. If enjoying company at a bar, you are in need of good companionship.

BASEMENT: See Cellar.

BASIN: A basin of cold water indicates the need to be closer to the family; a need for more warmth between you. A basin of warm water shows that you are loving and caring. A basin of dirty water means there will be family quarrels.

BASKET: If you are carrying a full basket, you will be offered a better paying job. If the basket is empty, you will lose your present job.

BAT: A bat flying around means that all your small problems will be cleared up very quickly and easily. If the bat is at rest, hanging upside down, then what seem like small problems now may later develop into big ones.

BATH: To dream of filling a bath with water is a warning against throwing your money down the drain. If you are taking a bath, you are in need of a vacation. If you are in a bath with other people (or a sauna, or hot tub) you should be cautious of business dealings. If you are bathing in dirty water, people are going to gossip.

BATTLEFIELD: See Army.

BAYONET: A symbol for caution. If you stab someone with a bayonet, be careful in your dealings with the opposite sex. If you are stabbed with a bayonet, you will suffer financial loss.

BEAR: Great hidden strength. If you kill a bear, you will overcome seemingly insurmountable odds. If you are chased by a bear, you will have many business problems and will have to deal with unpleasant people. If you track or hunt a bear, you will gain in stature and be greatly respected.

BEARD: Dreaming that you wear a beard, when in fact you don't, means that you are very much an individualist and don't care too much about what others think of you.

BED: A neatly made bed means security. An unmade bed means secrets will be discovered. If you are in bed alone, it indicates loneliness. If you are in bed with someone of the same sex, you will have to apologize for your actions. If you are in bed with someone of the opposite sex, you will have to make a big decision. If you are in a bed that is outdoors, or the bed is empty but outdoors, there is the opportunity to earn a great deal of money. See also Featherbed.

BEE: Profit; gain. If the bees fly away, you will be rid of your worries. To be stung by a bee means you will be severely reprimanded.

BEEHIVE: Success in business. If you knock over the hive, you will be in for a lawsuit.

BEGGAR: Opportunities. To give freely to the beggar means you will be making great gains and having tremendous opportunities. To ignore a beggar is to miss out on what could bring you big success. See also Meeting.

BELLOWS: You will be having company. If you are pumping the bellows, it means that the coming company will cause a lot of work for you.

BELLS: Gypsies believe that bells generally signify misfortune. A single, tolling bell is a sign of approaching death, or of serious illness. A peal of bells, however, is a sign of coming celebration. A persistent doorbell is an alarm . . . you should be on your guard.

BENCH: To dream of sitting on a bench is a warning not to speak too openly about your private affairs to people you don't know too well.

BICYCLE: To dream of riding a bicycle means that you are becoming automatic in the work you do. You need to step back and look at the whole picture, giving yourself inspiration to become more creative.

BILLIARDS/POOL: To see an empty billiard or pool table means you will be lucky in love. To play the game means that someone is going to be lying to you, or you to them.

BIRD: Birds, in general, mean success. Flying birds indicate a coming journey. To have a bird land on your hand, arm, or head means an unexpected love is coming into your life. To kill a bird, or find a dead bird, is an ill omen. Gypsies in different parts of England have different ideas about dreams concerning specific birds. Following are a few of those ideas:

Blackbird: A need for caution. Examine all business matters carefully.

Canary: Death of a friend. A sudden departure. A flying canary means temporary sickness.

Crow: You will be disappointed in an expectation and will have to make do with what you have.

Dove: Fidelity in love; happiness at home. A flock of doves means an abundance of love and happiness. Two doves together mean reconciliation.

Eagle: A soaring eagle indicates great business success.

Falcon/Hawk: A soaring falcon or hawk, as with an eagle, means business success. A swooping falcon or hawk means success in a legal matter. To carry the bird on your arm and/or release it means to branch out, embracing new associates in your business or personal life.

Lark: A short vacation, with fun and relaxation.

Nightingale: To hear or see a nightingale is the forerunner of joyful news, great success in business, joy in love. To hear a nightingale sing is to be assured of happiness.

Owl: You must give great thought to a coming problem, rather than making a snap decision. If the owl flies away, you will find the problem is not as big as it seems. To hear an owl hoot is to be warned of coming problems.

Parrot: Beware of slander. Don't listen to gossip.

Peacock: To dream of a peacock is a sign of popularity, but beware of pride and vanity. If it is a peacock which suddenly spreads its tail, beware of ostentation. To hear a peacock scream means there is an approaching storm that will do you some damage. This could be a domestic or business "storm."

Pigeon: To dream of a flying pigeon, according to Gypsies in Yorkshire, is to expect news in the form of a letter. If you don't see the pigeon land, it could be good or bad news. If you see the bird land, then it is definitely good news.

Raven A favorite bird of the Gypsies. Many dream books call this a bird of ill omen, but Romanis say that to dream of it signifies a family reunion with much happiness and joy to come. If it is flying, the reunion will be unexpected; if at rest, it will be something you organize.

Swallow: Flying swallows mean happiness and good fortune. Nesting swallows mean close friendship.

Swan: You will have a happy and contented family life. If there are young signets with the swan(s), then you will have children.

Vulture: Represents a bitter enemy. To kill a vulture is to triumph over your enemy. To see one devouring its prey is a warning about a lawsuit.

BIRD'S NEST: A sign of coming marriage. A nest full of eggs means success in your personal life. A nest full of baby birds presages a coming trip with friends. An empty nest means that plans for a trip will fall through. See Bird for individual bird nests.

BIRTHDAY PARTY: See Christmas Party.

BISCUIT: See Eating/Drinking.

BISHOP: You will receive news of the death of a distant relative. See also Abbot.

BLACKBIRD: See Bird.

BLACKBOARD: See Chalk.

BLACKSMITH: You will be very successful through your own hard work.

BLIND PERSON: See Meeting.

BLINDFOLD: To have a blindfold placed over your eyes means you are seeking knowledge. To blindfold someone else means you have knowledge that you should be giving to someone else.

BLOOD: The Gypsies say that to dream of blood on your hands means you will receive an inheritance. To see a pool of blood means there is the opportunity for an investment that could pay off very well.

BLOSSOM: To see trees in blossom indicates that you will have good luck in the future. The work you do now will be well rewarded, though you may have to wait a while to see the results. One old Gypsy woman insisted that the only meaning for dreaming of blossoms (she specified fruit tree blossoms) was a coming wedding. See also Orange Blossom.

BLUE: See Colors.

BOAR: Beware of business associates. If you dream of being chased by a boar, you will encounter a bitter enemy. To go on a boar hunt is to labor uselessly. To kill a boar is to gain a victory over your enemies.

BOAT/SHIP: To dream of a sailboat is to be complacent. However, if it is in stormy seas, then you are going to find yourself extremely busy. A sailboat is also a means of transport and, as such, should be considered as another form of symbolizing spiritual progression. It would be of a lighter, almost dilettante form. A steamship, another method of transportation, would be a slow but steady form. A lifeboat is not transportation per se, so it may symbolize a need to escape; trying to get out of a difficult situation. See also individual boat types.

BOILED MEAT: See Eating/Drinking.

BONES: See Skeleton.

BOOKS: See Library.

BOOTS/SHOES: New boots or shoes mean you will have good luck in business, possibly connected with a trip out of town. Old, worn boots or shoes indicate worries, and can mean separation from loved ones.

BOSOM: A well-developed, shapely bosom or breast indicates that you have wealth and comfort to look forward to. If the breasts are old and withered, then you will experience sadness and, possibly, illness.

BOTTLE: To dream of a full bottle is symbolic of having plenty and being willing to share with others. To see an empty bottle symbolizes a need; a yearning.

BOUQUET: A sign of love. To have a bouquet presented to you is to have love offered to you. If you are the one presenting the bouquet, then you will be meeting someone who attracts you very much. To carry a bouquet means an approaching marriage. To catch a bouquet thrown at you means you will meet your true love. To throw a bouquet indicates displeasure. Faded flowers in a bouquet mean there will be sickness.

BOW: See Shooting.

BOX: To dream of a box or boxes full of items indicates that you will be taking a journey. To dream of empty boxes means you will lose something which, although you seldom used it, was important to you.

BOY: Gypsies say that to dream of a young boy is a sure sign of pleasures to come, both in business and in home life. If the boy is older—in his early teens—then it is a sign that hard work will bring great reward.

BRACELET: A bracelet around the wrist means you will inherit a legacy. Worn higher up the arm, you will receive a gift. An ankle bracelet means you will frivolously spend an inheritance. To lose a bracelet is to let an opportunity slip through your fingers.

BREAST: See Bosom.

BRIDE: To dream of a bride indicates wealth to come. A young girl dreaming of a bride will find her true love. To kiss a bride is to be assured of an increase in wealth.

BRIDGE: To cross a bridge means you will overcome your difficulties. If the bridge is old, you will overcome them, but it will take much work on your part. If the bridge is new and strong, you will have an easy time of it.

BRIDLE: A bridle on a horse means that you are being manipulated.

BROOK/STREAM: Social advancement. If it is rough water, there is the possibility of social gaffes and gossip. See also River.

BROOM: If you are sweeping with a broom, you need to change your habits; possibly change your friends (certainly examine them and whether or not they are good for you). To see a broom standing in a corner means that you must examine your way of life to see if you are living up to your full potential.

BROWN: See Colors.

BUCKET: To dream of a bucket full of water or other liquid means that you will receive something to your advantage. If the bucket is empty, you will be given an opportunity to gain something.

BULL: The Romani belief is that to dream of a bull means you are going to experience financial gain. If it is a white bull, then it will be a gain in love and friendship. To be chased by a bull means you should be careful in your business dealings. To fight a bull or be at a bull-fight means there are many different forces at work and you need to concentrate your efforts on one particular path of advancement.

BURGLARS: Precarious money matters. Check into your investments and be sure they are sound.

BURIAL: The end of an episode in your life. Time for a new beginning. Start looking about you and consider the path you want to take. See also Funeral.

BURN: To burn any object symbolizes ridding yourself of something that is unwanted. To burn yourself is to chastise yourself for something you know you have done wrong.

BUST: See Bosom.

BUTCHER: Seeing or watching a butcher cut up meat means you must be careful not to cause gossip about your actions. To see a butcher slaughter an animal presages the death of a relative.

BUTTER: See Eating/Drinking.

BUTTERFLY: Your lover is popular and a flirt, but nothing more. In other words, he or she may flirt, but remains always faithful to you.

CAB/TAXI: To ride in a cab is to have good fortune. Some Romanis say it indicates that a short but pleasant vacation is coming.

CAGE: You have things well under control. If you are in the cage, you will be visited by relatives you do not care for.

CALF: Seeing a calf at a cow's udder is a sign that you will achieve your ambitions. If a young woman dreams of seeing a young calf, it means her husband will be a good provider.

CAMEL: Good things coming into your life. If you dream of a caravan of camels, then it will be money that is coming.

CAMEO BROOCH: You will achieve a position of importance, with people working under you.

CAMPGROUND: The Romani *atchin' tan* symbolizes a grand reunion to come, with much celebration and enjoyment. You will be getting together with people you haven't seen for a long time—friends and relatives—and exchanging news and gossip.

CANAL: To dream of a boat on a canal signifies that your love life will become complicated. If a horse pulls the boat, however complicated it becomes, it will eventually even out and flow smoothly again.

CANARY: See Bird.

CANDLE: An unlit candle is a symbol of opportunity. A lit candle symbolizes revelation; that which was hidden will be revealed to you. To dream of a candelabra or chandelier is a sign of taking on new responsibility.

CANNON: A firing cannon means achievement; accomplishment. A stationary cannon, with the cannonballs piled beside it, means opportunity.

CANOE: Success in love. If you are in a canoe that tips over, you will have a quarrel with your lover.

CAPON: See Eating/Drinking.

CAPE: To be wearing a cape means you are trying to cover up some action of which you are ashamed.

CAPTAIN: To be captain of a ship is to be in command, so to dream of being a captain means that you will have major decision(s) to make, which could affect many people. To meet with a ship's captain means that you will be able to influence whomever is in the position to make a decision.

CAR: See Automobile.

CARAVAN: See Camel.

CARDINAL: See Abbot. Also see Meeting.

CARDS, PLAYING: Symbolize life, according to Romanis. If you dream you are winning when playing cards, you will do well and profit in life. If you are losing, you will suffer some setbacks. If you are shuffling cards, there will be decisions to make. If cards are dealt to you, you will find yourself with a sudden problem to solve.

CAROUSEL: You will have many opportunities, any one of which could be advantageous. Choose one and stick with it; don't keep changing your mind.

CARPET/RUG: A rich ornamental or oriental carpet means you will receive riches. An old and worn carpet means you will fall on hard times.

CARRIAGE/WAGON/VARDO: The vardo is the Gypsies' house-on-wheels. If you dream of a vardo or wagon approaching you, there are people coming to visit you, or bringing news to you (which could be good or bad). If the wagon is going away, you will be parted from a loved one. A stationary or passing wagon means things will stabilize and not change for some time. If you are riding in the wagon, you are making progress (and again consider the spiritual connotations, with this being a means of transportation). If you are driving the wagon yourself, you are in charge of your own life and able to make the decisions.

CASTANETS: You will suffer many minor irritations.

CASTLE: Ambition. You have high ideals and a great desire to advance yourself. Some Gypsies say that to dream of castles can also mean a coming journey that will take you where you have never been before. It could lead to adventure, opportunity, mystery. Be ready for anything!

CAT: A sleeping cat means that someone is plotting against you. A cat washing itself means you need to get your affairs in order. A cat walking or running is a sign of missed opportunity. If a cat scratches you, you will be involved in a lawsuit. To hear a cat's meow is to be warned of coming unpleasantness.

CATERPILLAR: Beware of false friends.

CAVALRY: An opportunity to make a great deal of money, if you are very careful. If the cavalry is charging, you will get a promotion in your work.

CAVE/CAVERN: To see a cave or cavern means there will be an opportunity to go back and correct something you have done wrong. To be inside a cavern is to have security, if only for a short while.

CELLAR: If you open the door to a cellar, you will uncover a lot of unsavory gossip. If you find yourself down in a cellar, you are mixing with undesirable company.

CEMETERY: A well-kept cemetery, with flowers on the graves, indicates that you will have many friends who will be faithful to you for many years. An unkempt cemetery indicates loss of friends; acquaintances rather than close friends.

CHAIN: A restriction. To be bound in chains is to be held back from doing what you want to do. See also Dress.

CHAIR: See types of chairs.

CHALK: A stick of chalk or any chalked writing on a blackboard indicates a temporary advantage that could as easily slip away again. If it is writing, take note of what is written.

CHALLENGE: If you are challenged by another, you will be involved in an argument with the opposite sex. If you are the one who issues the challenge, you will argue with someone of your own sex.

CHANDELIER: See Candle.

CHECKERS: Playing checkers indicates you will be involved in an argument with others. See also Chess.

CHEESE: See Eating/Drinking.

CHERRIES: See Fruits.

CHESS: Playing chess indicates you will be involved in an argument with family members. See also Checkers.

CHESTNUT/CHESTNUT TREE: Dreaming of a chestnut means you will be healthy and strong. A chestnut tree indicates you will have sons. See also Tree.

CHICKEN: See Hen.

CHILD: See Baby. See also Meeting.

CHIMES: See Bells.

CHIMNEY: The Gypsies say that dreaming of a chimney that is not smoking means you are in need of a sexual outlet. A smoking chimney means you are involved in an affair. See also Smoke.

CHINA DISHES/POTTERY: Personal property will be stolen.

CHOIR: To dream that you are singing in a choir means that you will do something for others that will earn you great respect.

CHRISTMAS PARTY/BIRTHDAY PARTY: To be at a party means that you will be meeting with your lover the following day, and will have a wonderful time.

CHRISTMAS TREE: You will have a large family.

CHURCH: You are going to receive some bad news. If you are inside the church, you are going to become very depressed and very pessimistic.

CHURCHYARD: To dream of a churchyard means you will soon find yourself in a lawyer's office.

CIGARETTE: See Smoke.

CIRCUS: To dream of a circus means you are going to be so active in both your social and business life, that you won't have time to do many of the things you would really like to do.

CLOCK: Seeing a clock on a building signifies that you will receive some recognition. A small clock indicates that you have to reach a quick decision. To wind a clock means you have much work to do to get a reasonable return. To hear a clock chiming is a warning that time is running out. If possible, try to remember the time shown on a clock in your dreams (or the number of times it strikes). This could be significant—see Numbers. See also Alarm Clock.

COBWEB: A sign of laziness, unless there is also a spider present. See also Spider.

COCK: Pride, success, power. Fighting cocks mean there will be a challenge to your position.

COFFIN: Generally a good sign. The Gypsies say that to see someone lying in a coffin means that you will live to see your children grown and married. To see yourself in a coffin means you will enjoy excellent health throughout your life. But, to see someone famous in a coffin means the possibility of war.

COLORS:

Blue: Gypsies associate the color blue with the sky; dark blue with the night sky. They say that to have that color especially prominent in a dream indicates a desire to get out into the open, to get away. Perhaps a need for a vacation.

Brown: The color of the earth. A need to get down to your roots, or to the basics of your problems.

Green: The color of grass. When green is prominent in your dreams, it indicates growth and abundance.

Orange: The color for life and new beginnings (perhaps tied in with the sunrise).

Purple: A color of richness and luxury.

Red: The universal color for danger and excitement.

Yellow: Many Gypsy vardos are painted yellow. It's a color for happiness, and for love and family togetherness.

COMET: To see a comet rush across the sky means you will be having unexpected good fortune.

COMPASS: To dream of a compass means you are uncertain as to which direction you should proceed.

COMPUTER: Working at a computer in your dream means that you will have access to much information, including many secrets you have long tried to discover. Your immediate actions could have far-reaching effects.

If the computer's screen is blank, then it signifies frustration. If someone else is working at the computer, then you should be wary of giving out information you would rather keep to yourself. See also Internet.

CONCERT: If you attend or play at a concert, you will be able to play a musical instrument. If the music in the dream is terrible and off-key, then you will have arguments with relatives.

CONFETTI: You will have an exciting experience with someone who seems very glamorous to you.

CONVENT: There will be restrictions imposed upon you. See also Nun/Nunnery.

COOKIE: See Eating/Drinking.

CORKSCREW: You have a very inquisitive friend who could cause you harm.

CORONATION: You will earn a lot more money, but the increased wealth will bring with it far greater responsibility.

CORPSE: Another of those reverse symbols. If you are the corpse, you will be assured of a long, happy, and healthy life. If someone you don't know is the corpse, you will have a long and interesting life (not necessarily happy nor healthy).

COTTAGE/HOUSE: To dream of a cottage or house means that you will live a sedate life; quite happy but with no great excitement in it.

COW: A sign of home and comfort. You will want for little. If you are milking the cow, then you will have to work hard most of your life but will be well rewarded for it.

CRAB: Signifies the possibility of a lawsuit with someone you thought of as a friend.

CRADLE: If there is a child in the cradle, then you will have a child. If the cradle is empty, it means you will be relocating.

CRICKET: To dream of seeing a cricket or hearing a cricket chirring foretells long life and happy times ahead.

CROCODILE/ALLIGATOR: You will have an accident, brought about by trying to avoid your enemies.

CROQUET: Playing croquet means you will have a very pleasant time with close friends.

CROSS: An equal-armed cross is a sign of good luck to come. If the cross is enclosed in a circle, it means there will be financial good luck.

CROSSROADS: You will have a decision to make that could affect the rest of your life.

CROW: See Bird.

CROWN: A warning. Be very careful in all decisions you make, especially business decisions. If it is a paper crown (as at a party), you are heading for a fall.

CRUCIFIX: You will experience shame and humiliation.

CRYING: See Tears.

CURLS: If you dream you have curly hair, you will be much sought after on the social scene, and much admired by the opposite sex. If it is someone else who has the curls, beware of criticizing others, especially the opposite sex. If curls are cut off, you will suddenly find yourself without friends. See also Hair.

CURTAINS (LACE): Frivolity. You may have a light affair, or you may indulge in a little gambling.

DAFFODILS: Sign of an early marriage.

DAGGER: If you are holding the dagger, you are going to antagonize someone. If you are not holding the dagger, it will be someone you do not wish to harm. See also Knife.

DAISIES: White daisies indicate a faithful spouse. Yellow daisies show a spouse's jealousy due to your receiving too much attention from someone else.

DANCING: See Ballroom.

DANDELIONS: Represent false friends. If there are a lot of dandelions . . . watch out!

DAUGHTER: You are going to be very worried over the actions of someone else, but your worries will turn out to be needless.

DEAD: See Corpse.

DEAF: If you dream that you are deaf, it means you will quickly be relieved of all your worries. If you are trying to talk to someone who is deaf, you will experience a number of minor irritations.

DEATHBED: To be on your deathbed means you will soon receive a visit from someone you haven't seen in a very long time. To be at someone else's deathbed means you will be going to visit someone you haven't seen in a long time.

DEBT: To dream you are in debt means you will receive money from an older relative.

DECANTERS: The number of decanters indicates the number of children you will have. Full decanters indicate girls; empty or only partially full decanters indicate boys.

DECISION: To ponder on a problem and then reach a decision means that you will start a new project or a new job, or relocate.

DEER: A female deer is a sign of hard times to come. An antlered deer means you are in for a long, hard battle. See also Stag and Fawn.

DELAY: When there seems to be a long delay in your dream, with you waiting for something to happen, it means that you will receive a surprise that could be pleasant or unpleasant.

DENTIST: To dream you are at the dentist means that you will have a sudden change of fortune. To have a tooth extracted means you will meet a new love.

DESERT: To find yourself in a desert is a sign that you are searching for knowledge.

DESK: If the desk is cluttered, you need to reorganize things in your life and get a system of priorities. If the desk is bare, you should look for new interests, new hobbies. See also Writing Desk.

DEVIL: A devil (*Beng* is the Romani word) appearing in your dreams is an indication that your friends are insincere.

DEW: Romanis say that it is a very good omen to dream that you see the dew on the early morning grass. It indicates that you will be lucky in love and that your life will always be happy.

DIAMOND: A single diamond is an indication of social success. A number of diamonds, as in a necklace or brooch, mean a long, happy marriage.

DICE: A die or dice being cast is a sign of family worries to come. Throwing a lucky combination indicates short-lived happiness.

DINNER: To dine alone or with your lover means you will be forgiving someone or receiving forgiveness from someone. To dine with a number of people denotes petty bickering and quarreling.

DISABLED PERSON: See Meeting.

DISEASE: Whether it's you or someone else afflicted by disease, in the dream it applies to you. Many times such dreams are warning you that you are on a course of self-destruction. Examine your lifestyle, your eating habits, your health care, and change them if necessary.

DISHES: See China Dishes.

DITCH: Deceit; trouble. Be cautious. To fall into a ditch is a warning of coming injury.

DIVING BELL/SUIT: To be submerged beneath the sea in a diving bell or diving suit signifies that you will find yourself in a predicament over which you have no control, but which you will nonetheless find fascinating.

DOCK: See Port.

DOCTOR: Watch your health if you dream of a doctor. (The Romani word for doctor is *mullomengro* which, literally translated, means "dead man maker.") You are susceptible to any colds or flus (or worse) that may be around. This is true whether you dream of meeting with a doctor or if you are the doctor yourself. See also Meeting.

DOG: To play with a dog is to expect to suffer from former extravagance. To be chased by a dog is to lose a friend. A running dog means there will be loss from a lawsuit. A barking dog indicates that you will become close friends with people you had previously tended to mistrust. To be bitten by a dog means you'll have an argument with your spouse. To hear a dog barking is a warning of danger to come.

DOMINOES: Beware of any form of investment presented to you.

DONKEY: See Ass.

DOOR: See Backdoor.

DOVE: See Bird.

DRAGON: A dragon symbolizes a dangerous undertaking. If you slay a dragon, you achieve great success.

DRAGONFLY: You'll be taking a short trip by air.

DRAPERIES: Rich and luxurious draperies are reflected in your life, which will be rich and luxurious. But old, torn drapes indicate great hardships to come. See also Curtains (Lace).

DRESS (WHITE): To dream of a woman in a white dress or, if a woman, to dream of wearing a white dress, portends that you will be accused of some malicious gossip but will be proven innocent.

DRESS, ARTICLES OF:

Chain: A chain belt, or similar article of dress, denotes union.

Embroidery: Love that could grow to something wonderful.

Fan: Pride, touched with vanity.

Feathers: White: a great sense of humor. Black: a pessimistic attitude. Also see Feather.

Garter: A symbol of rank and recognition. You will be promoted, but this will place you in a more vulnerable position. You will have to be much more careful in considering the consequences of your words and actions.

Gauze: Affected modesty.

Gloves: Pleasure to come that will be all too brief.

Hat: A new hat is the sign of a surprise. A hat that is too big is a sign of ostentation. A hat too small shows that you are overly modest.

Linen: Fortune; abundance.

Muff: Ostentation. You too often do things on a whim.

Needles: Disappointment in love.

Pearls: Tears.

Pins: Contradiction.

Ribbons: Change of employment.

Sash: To be wearing a sash means that you will be singled out for some sort of recognition, but that it will cause jealousy among your friends.

Satin/Silk: Financial gain.

Shoes: See Boots.

Veil: You have something to hide.

Velvet: To dream of black velvet is a portent of a coming death. Purple velvet signifies glory and luxury to come. Red velvet is a dangerous affair that could lead to scandal. Blue velvet is a need for a vacation. Green velvet is a sign of unexpected wealth.

DRINKING GLASS: To see a number of drinking glasses means there will be sudden arguments between you and your lover. A single glass indicates the need for a short vacation. To break a glass means that you are going to have to suddenly change plans you have made.

DROWNING: If you are drowning, it means you will be shamed. If someone else is drowning, you will be involved in a minor scandal.

DRUGS: Taking drugs is a sign of dependency, which can easily get out of control. Carefully review any medications you may be taking. If the dream indicates that you should be taking a particular drug, check with your doctor to see if it is something you are actually lacking.

DRUM: A sign of communication. If you are beating a drum, you will write an important letter. If you hear a drum being beaten, you will receive an important letter.

DRUNK: See Intoxication.

DUCK/GOOSE: A generally favorable omen. A quacking duck or goose is the herald of good news to come. To shoot a duck is to make a mistake, to "stick your foot in it." To see a duck or ducks flying overhead means good news is coming if they fly from left to right, and bad news if they fly from right to left.

DUEL: Indicates that you are unsure of a recent decision that you made. Whether or not you win the duel will indicate whether or not you were right in that decision.

DUNGEON: To be locked up in a dungeon means you are being controlled by others.

DWARF: See Meeting.

EAGLE: See Bird.

EARRING(S): To be wearing one earring means you will be with the one you love. To be wearing two earrings means you will be flirting with a number of people.

EARTHQUAKE: You are very unsure of yourself and need to do something to gain a little self-confidence.

EASY CHAIR: You have been working too hard and deserve a vacation.

EATING/DRINKING:

    Bacon: To slice bacon indicates the coming death of a loved one. To eat bacon means triumph over enemies. If you are smoking or curing bacon, someone close to you will become ill.

Biscuit/Cookie: There will be great rejoicing.

Boiled or Roast Meat: You will tend to be melancholy and dwell a lot on the past.

Brandy: Indicative of living "high off the hog" with little thought for tomorrow and little regard for your friends.

Bread: To smell bread means you will be given an opportunity to make some money. A loaf of bread handed to you could mean a new child on the way. To slice bread is to divide up your luck into small amounts. To eat fresh bread is to enjoy good friendship. To eat stale bread is to open yourself up to possible sickness.

Butter: You will have good fortune mixed with sadness. Wealth to come, but at a price.

Cabbage: To dream of eating cabbage means you will receive good luck. To dream of cooking cabbage means you will go into debt.

Cake: Eating cake means good luck. Strangely, if a woman dreams she is eating wedding cake, it means she will have a period of bad luck. To make and bake a cake means you will bring your own luck.

Capon: You have been deceived in your affections.

Champagne: Symbolizes money. A bottle of champagne is the chance to make money. To drink champagne is to receive money. To toast a newly married couple with champagne is to be assured of success in business.

Cheese: Vexation; frustration, but final success.

Chocolate: Eating or drinking chocolate means that you will soon be going through an illness, though not a serious one.

Coffee: To drink or smell coffee is a sign of long life.

Corn: Corn on the cob indicates coming financial gain. Corn growing in a field means you will have a good and happy marriage. Popcorn means a sudden, unexpected windfall.

Cream: If you are drinking cream, you will receive an unexpected gift. If you spill cream, you will have to pay an unexpected bill.

Eeels: Malicious enemies.

Eggs: A wealth of family love.

Flour: To see flour, either packaged or at the mill, means it is a good time to invest, but don't put all your money into one thing.

Ham: You will meet a very jolly person.

Honey: You are being falsely sweet to someone and it shows!

Jam/Jelly: To dream of putting up jam preserves means you will develop good friends among your neighbors.

Lettuce: To dream of lettuce is good, according to the Gypsies. For a woman, it signifies a wonderful time to come with her lover(s). For a man, it signifies the attention of a number of beautiful women.

Liquor/Liquers: You may do something you will very much regret afterwards.

Macaroni: A symbol of great distress.

Milk/Milking: To dream of drinking milk indicates you will be very lucky in love. To dream of milking a cow means you will have to work at winning the person you desire, but you will eventually be successful.

Millet: A sign of poverty.

Mustard: There will be a number of family quarrels.

Oysters: To dream that you are eating oysters is a very favorable sign, usually signifying a large family. If you are married, your spouse will be very much in love with you and you will have several children; if you are not married, you soon will be and then will go on to have children.

Pancakes: Seeing, cooking, or eating pancakes means that some of the things you presently think of as curses in your life are going to turn out to be blessings.

Pastry: To be eating pastries means you will miss an important appointment. You could suffer illness at a most inconvenient time.

Rice: As with millet, a sign of poverty.

Salad: Various embarrassments.

Salmon: A sign of deceit. To eat salmon means you will discover the deceiver.

Salt: You will be recognized for great wisdom.

Sausages: You will be accused of interfering in some one else's love affair.

Soup: You will return to good health.

Vinegar: You will labor in vain for a while.

Wine: To dream that you are drinking wine is a good omen. It prognosticates health, wealth, long life, and happiness. If you are in love, you will marry the person you adore. If you are married, you will draw especially close to your spouse.

ECHO: To hear your voice echoing means that you are being mocked behind your back.

ECLIPSE: Of the sun—denotes coming loss. Of the moon—means profit.

EELS: See Eating/Drinking.

EGGS: See Eating/Drinking.

ELECTIONS: You have choices ahead of you. Although you may think that what you decide will make no difference, in fact it will. Look at any and all decisions that have to be made and choose carefully. However insignificant a decision may seem, it can have far-reaching effects.

ELEPHANT: A symbol of power. To ride one, you have the power. To see one pass by, you will be in touch with power and may be able to make use of it.

EMBRACE/HUG: If it is an affectionate one, it denotes a happy home life. If it is a passionate one, you should beware of your feelings getting out of hand.

EMBROIDERY: See Dress.

ENGINE: To dream of a railroad locomotive or steam engine means that you have the ability to do anything you wish. You can succeed at anything to which you put your mind. See also Train.

ENVELOPE: To address an envelope means you will soon meet with that person. If you receive an envelope, you will have an opportunity. If you mail an envelope, you will do someone a favor which they will appreciate and later repay. See also Letters and Address.

EPITAPH: You will make an indiscretion.

ERRAND: If you send someone else on an errand, you are fearful that your spouse is being unfaithful. If you are sent on an errand, you are planning on being unfaithful.

EXECUTION: To witness an execution means that you are thinking of divorcing your spouse or leaving your lover. To be the one about to be executed means you are feeling guilty about infidelities.

EXPLOSIONS: If you dream of explosions connected with quarrying, tunneling, etc., you have a lazy streak and would rather avoid work. If you dream of explosions that destroy buildings and people, you are afraid of firm commitments, especially where love is concerned.

EYEPATCH: Shows an interest in the occult; things secret.

FALCON: See Bird.

FALLING: Falling dreams are not uncommon. The Gypsies say they indicate that you are unhappy, especially with personal relationships, and want to get out of a situation.

FALSE TEETH: To see false teeth, or someone noticeably wearing false teeth, means that someone is putting up a false front in dealing with you. Check your business contacts carefully. If you dream that you are wearing false teeth, it means that you are not being totally honest in things you are saying.

FAME: To dream of being famous means that you have high expectations but are in for big disappointments.

FAMINE: A sign of guilt about your spending. You unconsciously feel that while you are being extravagant, others are starving.

FAN: See Dress.

FARMER/FARM: As a result of your hard work, you will reap a fine reward. However, if you dream of a farm that is rundown, it forebodes financial losses.

FAT/FATNESS: To dream that you are fat is an unconscious acknowledgement that you are overeating.

FAUCET: A dripping faucet means you are wasting money in small amounts, but consistently. A running faucet means you are throwing away a great deal of money. A faucet that is turned off means you must exercise caution, for there is a possibility that you will be tempted to spend more money than you can afford.

FAWN: You will shortly meet with a wonderful person whom you will desire very much.

FEAST: Tremendous success financially. You will receive far more than you ever expected. See also Eating/Drinking.

FEATHER: A white feather means good luck coming your way. A black feather means financial loss. To see a number of feathers floating in the air, whatever their color, means you will have a chance to fulfill your desires. A large number of ostrich feathers is a sign of prosperity, but this is not necessarily accompanied by happiness. See also Dress.

FEATHERBED: Easy times ahead.

FENCE: To dream of a fence means you feel restricted. To climb over a fence means you are desperate to get out of a particular situation.

FERRY: A ferryboat shows that you will have the opportunity to bring two divided parties together.

FIELDS: If the fields are overgrown and wild, you will lose control of things unless you get down to a lot of hard work. If the fields are ploughed, you will have a wonderful opportunity to "plant seeds." If the fields are rich with harvest, you will receive abundance.

FIGS: See Fruits.

FINGER: To dream of a finger pointing at you means that you have done something underhanded and are afraid of being found out.

FIRE: A low, smoldering fire shows that you are repressing some strong desire. A blazing fire means that things are getting out of hand. If you set a fire, you are planning to do something that could have a tremendous impact on your life. To put out a fire means that you will win over people who have been opposing you. If you are sitting by a campfire, you will find comfort and happiness.

FISH: To see a fish swimming indicates joy and success. To catch a fish means that there will be illness in the family. To eat a fish means you will fall sick.

FLAG: To dream you see a flag waving means you may be in great danger from enemies. To carry or raise a flag means you will receive some mark of distinction.

FLAME: See Fire.

FLATTERY: If someone unduly flatters you, the Gypsies say it means that you are feeling very good about yourself, but beware of becoming egotistical.

FLEAS: Small irritations. Small problems in your business and private affairs. See also Insects.

FLIES: Someone is jealous because of your success. To swat at flies is to irritate that person and flaunt your success. See also Insects.

FLIRT: If you are the one flirting, you are not happy in your present situation. If someone is flirting with you, you can expect a mild love affair to develop.

FLOWERS/GARLAND: A symbol for hope, especially where love is concerned. See also individual flower names.

FLUTE: The sound of a flute shows a happy home life. To play the flute shows love for your family.

FLYING: To dream that you are flying through the air (and most common is to dream that you are using a swimming motion to do this) indicates that you feel restricted. You want to be free to carry out your desires. The Gypsies say this is often tied in with sexual frustration. To dream of flying in an airplane is slightly different, indicating that you want to hurry things along; you are anxious to get somewhere much faster than you are going.

FOG/FOGHORN: Uncertainty. To dream that you are in a thick mist or fog means that your way in life will often seem dark and perplexing. But, by perseverance and by applying yourself to your own self-development, you will come out of the dark into the light. To be completely lost in a fog means you are frustrated, not knowing what decision to make. To hear a foghorn means that there are troubled times coming.

FOOD: See Eating/Drinking.

FOOTMAN: See Meeting.

FOREST: To be in a large, beautiful forest means you will find peace and tranquility. If you are lost in a forest, then you will have family quarrels.

FORTUNETELLING (*Dukkerin'*): To dream of having your fortune told indicates that you will have a sudden change of fortune that might be for the better or worse. If you are the fortuneteller, it means that you will be having flashes of insight into the future. Pay particular attention to any "hunches" you have in the next few days.

FOUNTAIN: A spouting fountain symbolizes a happy marriage. A small fountain is a sign of love that is capable of being developed into something wonderful. A fountain that dries up means that you are heading for the rocks where love is concerned.

FOX: Cleverness; cunning. If you see a fox passing by, you will be the clever one. If you are on a fox hunt, beware of others. A vixen with her cubs indicates a clever woman.

FROG: You will progress "by leaps and bounds," say the Gypsies! If you see a frog sitting still, it is not yet definite that you will be moving forward in the near future. If you see it jumping, then hold on!

FRUITS:

  Apples: Green apples indicate fickle friendships. Ripe red apples show true friendship you can depend upon. Baked apples or apples in a pie mean great expectations followed by disappointment. See also Apple.

  Apricots: Good health and contentment.

Cherries: Black cherries: deception by your lover. Red cherries: you can have complete trust in your lover.

Figs: If you see figs growing on a tree, you will encounter a foreigner who could be very good for you and/or your business. If you are eating figs, you will gain new knowledge.

Grapes: Rejoicing; celebration. To eat grapes means satisfaction with yourself and your work.

Lemons: Symbolize struggle. Lemons frequently indicate that you will marry someone of a sour disposition. If you dream of actually squeezing lemons, then you will have a hard struggle to make ends meet. To suck a lemon indicates a possible legal suit against you. To drink lemon juice is to be drawn into a court case.

Melons: Any sort of melon indicates a coming journey across water.

Nuts: Conjugal happiness. Eating nuts of any type means that you will gratify your sexual desires. To break open a nut means you will have a job getting what you want but, when you do get it, it will be well worth it.

Olives: Much like nuts, a sexual symbol. Black olives indicate you will enjoy sexual favors with someone you already know and will spend time with close friends. Green olives indicate you will enjoy sexual favors with someone you do not yet know, and will make new friends.

Oranges: Signify amusement. To eat oranges means you will be well entertained.

Peaches: Presage a journey over land.

Pears: You will be unexpectedly invited to a party.

Plums: Unchanging friendship. Someone whose loyalty you were wondering about will prove to be true.

Pomegranates: Symbols of sexual power. To dream of eating pomegranates means you will sexually dominate the opposite sex.

Strawberries: Unexpected good fortune, both in the home and in business.

FUNERAL: News of the death of someone not close to you. The death will indirectly benefit you. An unexpected inheritance. See also Burial.

GAG: To dream that your mouth is gagged or covered in some way means that you will be kissed in the near future.

GAMBLING: You are not satisfied with the direction your life is taking. You want to make changes just for the sake of changing, even if they are reckless changes. See Chaper 6, "Dreaming for Profit."

GARLAND: See Flowers.

GARLIC: Symbolizes prosperity.

GAS: To dream that you smell gas means that you have false friends. To see a high, bright gas flame means that you will have a love affair with a rich person. If the flame is low, the affair will be with a person who will involve you in scandal.

GATE: To find your way blocked by a closed gate means you will be frustrated in your desires. If the gate is open and you can pass through, then your plans will go fairly smoothly with only minor hitches.

GAUZE: See Dress.

GHOST: To see a ghost means a distant relative is displeased with you. To see the ghost of someone you know often presages the death of that person (though not always).

GIANT: To dream of a giant means that you feel insecure and have an inferiority complex.

GIFT: A gift received from a man means the possibility of danger; received from a woman, it is a sign of spite. If you give the gift, you will be relieving yourself of problems and worries.

GLASS: See Drinking Glass.

GLOVES: See Dress.

GOAT: To dream of goats is a sign of prosperity. But if you get butted by a goat, you will suffer a loss. To be milking a goat means several small setbacks but final triumph.

GOGGLES: You will discover something to your advantage; something that your enemy hoped you would overlook.

GOLDFISH: You will break with your present lover, which will cause much heartache. But as a result of this, you will meet with someone far superior, who will bring you great joy, love, and happiness.

GOLD: To dream of gold means you have a tendency to be greedy. If you buy gold, you will lose friends because of this greed. But if you are mining gold, you will overcome the tendency.

GOLF: You will live a long life and will have the opportunity to correct many mistakes that you have made.

GOOSE: See Duck.

GRANDMOTHER: To dream of a grandmother, or *puri dai* as the Gypsies call her, means that you are in need of help and advice. The grandmother is the "old wise one" of the family. She is always consulted when big decisions are to be made that affect the whole tribe. If, in your dream, she gives you advice . . . follow it! She will not be wrong.

GRANDPARENT: See Meeting.

GRAPES: See Fruits.

GRASS: Deep, green grass is a sure sign of a coming marriage. Poor, worn grass is a sign of hardship to come.

GRASSHOPPER: A bad sign, usually signifying financial losses to come.

GRAVE/GRAVESTONES: See Cemetery.

GREEN: See Colors.

GUITAR: To hear the music of a guitar or to watch a guitar player means you will be made happy by the one you love. If you are the person playing the guitar, beware of people who would swindle you.

GUN: Guns are generally tied in with arguments and disagreements: small guns (such as handguns) are for small arguments; large guns for big arguments. If you hear a gunshot, an argument involving you will soon develop. If you shoot a gun, you will be the cause of the argument. If someone shoots a gun at you (regardless of whether they hit you or miss), it means you will be badly hurt by a coming argument. See also Shooting.

GUNPOWDER: There is a plot developing to overthrow you; to cast you out of an important position you hold. The plotters are people you had thought to be your friends. See also Powder Flask.

GYPSY: To dream of a Gypsy or Gypsies is a sure sign that you will be wandering or traveling in the near future. If you dream that you are a Gypsy, you will enjoy a wonderfully happy marriage. If you are with a group of Gypsies, you are going to a reunion. If you dream of a Gypsy telling your fortune (*dukkerin'*), listen to what she says; it is important.

HAIL: Symbolizes trouble and distress.

HAIR: To dream of short hair means unhappiness. Long hair is a sign of good fortune. If your hair is disheveled and unkempt, there are annoyances and arguments coming, while well groomed hair shows abundance. To cut your hair, or see someone have their's cut, means you are working against yourself; hurting yourself by your actions. See also Curls.

HAM: See Eating/Drinking.

HAMMER: Using a hammer indicates that you are being very determined and forceful . . . perhaps a little too forceful.

HAMMOCK: If you are lying in a hammock by yourself, it is a sign of selfishness. To be lying in one with someone of the opposite sex means you will be attending a social function.

HANDCUFFS: Your hands are tied! There is something you really want to do, but you are being prevented from doing it.

HANDKERCHIEF: If your lover gives you a handkerchief, it is a sign of faithfulness. To pick up a handkerchief that has been dropped is to pick up someone else's troubles. To blow your nose with a handkerchief means there will be news of sickness in the family.

HANGMAN: See Meeting.

HARE/RABBIT: To see a hare or rabbit sitting still means you will have the chance to increase your prosperity. A warren of rabbits means much increase in your fortunes. A black rabbit signifies a high risk situation with your finances. A white rabbit is a sign of a legacy.

HARNESS: A horse in a harness is a sign that someone has dominance and regulation over you, yet has your own betterment at heart. If you are putting a harness on a horse, then you are the one who is going to dominate.

HAT: See Dress.

HATCHET: See Axe.

HAWK: See Bird.

HAY: The possibility of an inheritance. To be mowing hay signifies that it will be money that you have earned.

HEADSCARF: See Bandana.

HEARSE: To see a hearse go by means that you will be starting a new job. To be riding or driving a hearse means you will be relocating.

HEDGES: The Gypsies say that to dream of hedges means you will be involved in some important discussions. The Romani word for a conference is *bouri-pennen,* which literally translates as "hedge gathering," from the fact that such a meeting often takes place along or under the hedgerow.

HEDGEHOG: See Porcupine.

HEN/CHICKEN: Profit; considerable gain. A hen with chicks means you will be granted a favor you have been seeking. A hen laying an egg is good fortune. To hear a clucking hen means consolation for some hurt. To feed chickens means you will suffer some minor annoyances.

HERMIT: See Meeting.

HILL: If you climb up a hill, you will succeed in your undertakings. If you stand and look at a hill, you will be met with a challenge. To stand on a hilltop means you will be in a secure, comfortable position.

HOBO/VAGRANT: You have set down your roots and will be staying where you presently live for a very long time.

HOE: You will enjoy good health and spirits for a long time to come, though some Gypsies claim it means profit from selling and trading.

HOLE: To see a hole means the possibility of an accident. However, to fall into a hole means your lover is very sweet and loving!

HOLLY: A person of the opposite sex will charm and captivate you, but you should beware for he or she has ulterior motives.

HONEY: See Eating/Drinking.

HONEYMOON: To dream you are on your honeymoon means there is going to be a "rude awakening" coming to you in the very near future. Be prepared for not-so-pleasant surprises.

HOOD: To dream of wearing a hood means you have something to hide.

HORSE: Good fortune, in business and in the home. A white horse or a grey one indicates prosperity. A black or brown one indicates power and position. To be mounting a horse indicates you will be well rewarded for work done. To shoe a horse is to be assured of comfort in your old age. A stallion represents sexual power. A mare is sexual fulfillment.

HORSEBACK RIDING: To dream of going horseback riding means that you will enjoy pleasure at the price of your good name.

HORSEMAN: See Meeting.

HOT ROD: To drive a hot rod is to relive your youth. You have a yearning to "let down your hair" and run wild for a while. Give in to it; give yourself a break from the everyday monotony.

HOUNDS: To dream of hounds in full cry means that you will have plenty on your table for the coming year.

HOUSE: See Cottage.

HUG: See Embrace.

HUNGER: Temporary poverty.

HURDY-GURDY: See Organ Grinder.

ICE: Symbolizes a betrayed confidence. Secrets you have shared have not remained secret. See also Icicles.

ICICLES: To dream that you see a number of long, bright icicles hanging down means that bright and beautiful prospects will be yours in the future. If you are single, you will marry someone who will make you very happy.

INCENSE: To burn or smell incense means that you will be taking an interest in New Age, metaphysical material.

INK: To be writing using a pen and ink means you will betray a confidence. To spill ink means you will be exposed.

INSECTS: To be bothered by small insects means that you are restless and need to change jobs or relocate. See also Flies and Fleas.

INTERNET: If you are on the Internet in your dream, it is an indication that you have the potential to achieve anything to which you put your mind. You will be able to make contact with people who are able to further your best interests. See also Computer.

INTERRACIAL MARRIAGE: A sign that a stranger from a far distance will be visiting you and will have a great influence in your life. See also Wedding.

INTOXICATION: To dream that you are drunk means that you should guard against reckless spending. To dream of meeting a drunk means you should beware of financial losses.

ISLAND: To see an island means that those you think are your friends are not really that close or caring. If you dream of being alone on an island, it is a sign of loneliness and frustration.

IVY: If you dream of ivy growing over a large area or spreading, you should get a medical check-up. The Gypsies say that this often indicates an unsuspected illness that is developing.

JACKASS: See Ass/Donkey.

JAIL: Dreaming of being in jail indicates a feeling of guilt for something you have done that was wrong, but that you hoped to get away with.

JESTER: To dream of watching a court jester means that you are embarrassed about something a close friend or relative has done. If you are the jester, then you are embarrassed about something you have done.

JEWELRY: See individual items.

JIG: To dream of dancing a jig is a sign that someone is in love with you. If you watch someone else dancing a jig, you will fall in love.

JILTED: To be jilted in your dreams means your lover is unfaithful to you. If you jilt someone, then you are planning on being unfaithful to your lover.

JOB: To dream of working at your job is frequently a sign of satisfaction and pride. But, if in the dream you are very unhappy or uncomfortable in the situation, it is a warning that you are over-stressed and probably over-worked. You need to take a vacation or take up a hobby that is totally different from your work situation. If you dream of losing your job, it reflects a loss of security. You might stand a chance of losing someone you love or of losing your home. To dream of getting a promotion shows a confidence in yourself, which, if reflected in your work, could lead to a promotion or increase in pay.

JOCKEY: Dreaming of a jockey in a horse race means that you feel you have many ideas but too little time in which to work at them.

JUDGE: See Meeting.

JUGGLER: You are of a very competitive nature.

KETTLE: A bright copper kettle (*kavvi*) signifies great domestic comfort. You will enjoy a very happy home life. If the kettle is black and cast iron, you will have many children and be very close to them. If the kettle is boiling and blowing out steam, you will receive good news from a relative.

KEYS: You are a practical and sensible person. To fit a key into a lock shows that you are very capable and adaptable.

KISS: This is another of those "opposites": if you dream you are kissing your lover, you are due for a quarrel. To be kissing someone you don't know means you will get into a fight. To kiss a child means you will be made to look foolish.

KITCHEN: A friend is coming to visit unexpectedly.

KITE: To dream of flying a kite means that you feel you are not up to your job.

KNAPSACK: A need to get away and be by yourself for a while. You need a vacation and/or a change of scenery.

KNEES: To see or admire someone's knees means you will meet an attractive stranger. To be down on your knees means you will shortly have to ask someone's forgiveness.

KNIFE: A sign of quarrels. A knife worn in the belt signifies a broken love affair. A closed jackknife or pocket knife means the quarrel will not be serious and will soon be patched up. See also Dagger.

KNITTING NEEDLES: Your lover will be very industrious in making your marriage a happy one. If you are the one knitting, then it is you on whom the bulk of the responsibility will fall to make the marriage a success.

KNOT(S): If you dream of tying knots in a rope you are making problems for yourself.

LABORER: See Meeting.

LADDER: You aspire to greater things; climbing a ladder shows you will achieve them. If you climb a ladder to enter a house through a window, you would not be averse to doing something illegal to get ahead! If you fall from a ladder, you may run afoul of the law.

LADY: See Meeting.

LAMB: To see lambs in a field means you will find inner peace and happiness.

LAMP/LANTERN: To see a lantern indicates that you will achieve a breakthrough on something that has been frustrating you. To light a lantern (or switch on a light) means you will be acting in a joint venture with a friend. To extinguish a lantern means you will breakup a partnership.

LARK: See Bird.

LAWYER: See Meeting.

LEATHER: Indicates a good, steady position; something you can rely upon.

LEAVES: If the leaves are green and healthy, your love life will blossom. If the leaves are brown and falling, your love life will be in the doldrums.

LEECH: You will have to face up to family obligations that you have been trying to avoid.

LEMON: See Fruits.

LEOPARD: Ostentation; gaudiness; pretension. To hunt and kill a leopard indicates you should check your taste in dress—you may not be as fashionable as you think!

LETTERS: You will make a discovery that will benefit you. To receive a letter containing good news means that you will have the opportunity to earn more money. To receive a letter containing bad news means that people are talking about you. If you are writing a letter, you will do something that you will later regret. To receive a love letter indicates that you will be meeting someone who will interest you very much. If you are writing a love letter, you will shortly have a brief, but very enjoyable love affair.

LIBRARY/BOOKS: If you see a whole library of books, it means you will be greatly appreciated by people you do business with. To read a book means that secrets will be revealed to you. To be given a book similarly means that you will be told a secret.

LIFEBOAT: To be rescued by a lifeboat means you will gain a position of importance in your community.

LIGHTHOUSE: You will be awarded a medal or given some recognition for services you have done.

LIGHTNING: Trouble brought about by a woman you have been close to (though not a relative). To see lightning strike a tree or a building means you will be involved in a court case brought by this woman. See also Rain and Thunder and Lightning.

LILIES: Joy; pleasure; great success in love.

LINEN: See Dress.

LION: You have great dignity and are much admired by others. A captive lion means lasting friendship. To be surprised by a lion indicates treachery on the part of a friend. To hear a lion roaring is a sign of opportunity to come.

LIZARD: You need to watch your health and your diet in particular. You have an unhealthy body.

LOAF: See Baker and Eating/Drinking (Bread).

LOCK: You are getting into something that is forbidden. Be very careful.

LOCKET: Signifies a long-term, affectionate relationship that will bring you great joy and happiness.

LOCKSMITH: See Meeting.

LOCOMOTIVE: See Engine and Train.

LOLLIPOP: You will receive an unexpected gift from an admirer of the opposite sex.

LOOKING GLASS: See Mirror.

LORD: See Meeting.

LOTTERY TICKET: You could be a winner! If you can see (and remember) the number, bet on it. If you are given a lottery ticket in your dream, you will become very successful.

LOVE LETTER: See Letter.

LOVEMAKING: If you watch others making love, your plans will be successful. If you are making love yourself, you will receive great satisfaction from what you plan to do.

LOVER: See Meeting.

MACKEREL: To dream of fishing for mackerel is a sure sign that you will be traveling in the near future. To dream of eating mackerel signifies that someone will be coming to visit you.

MACARONI: See Eating/Drinking.

MADNESS: To dream of being mad shows a feeling of restriction, of being unable to express yourself. Also see Asylum/Pyschiatric Hospital.

MAGAZINE: To dream you are reading a magazine means that if you apply yourself you will make great advances. To see a magazine rack or someone else reading a magazine, means that you will come into contact with someone who is able to help you advance.

MAGISTRATE: You have made some error, of which you are not aware. Go back over your previous day's work and double-check everything.

MAGNIFYING GLASS: To dream that you are looking at things through a magnifying glass means that you have overextended yourself financially.

MAID: To see a serving maid means that you will receive some good news. If you are the maid, then you will get bad news.

MAIL: See Letter

MAIL CARRIER: To see a mail carrier means that you will be negotiating with a salesperson. If you are the mail carrier, it means you have been overcharged for something you recently bought.

MANDOLIN: To see and hear a mandolin being played means you will enjoy an intimate, romantic time with someone you care for.

MANSION: Signifies that you feel you are worth far more than you are receiving. Try to better your position by asking either for a raise or for promotion.

MARBLES: Playing marbles means that you will visit someone you knew many years ago. If you watch others playing marbles, then you will be visited by someone from the past.

MARE: See Horse.

MARIONETTES: If you dream that you are a marionette, you are being manipulated. If you watch a marionette show, you are aware of the manipulation of someone else.

MARRIAGE: See Interracial Marriage and Wedding.

MATCHES: To see a number of matches means you will have many close friends (only one match—only one close friend). To strike a match presages the start of a new and exciting friendship. To blow out a match is the end of a long-standing friendship.

MATTRESS: Any problems you are presently going through will come to a speedy conclusion. You will soon be able to relax again.

MAYOR: See Meeting.

MAYPOLE: Dreaming of dancing around a Maypole is a sure sign of being in love.

MEAT: See Eating/Drinking.

MEDALS: To be awarded a medal or to be wearing one means that you will receive recognition for an accomplishment. To see someone else wearing a medal means you must try to curb feelings of jealousy.

MEETING: In many dreams, you meet with different types of people. Here are the meanings for some that can be significant. See also separate listings for some of these.

Baker: Symbolizes gain.

Beggar: Unexpected help from an unlikely source.

Blind Person: You have false friends.

Cardinal: You will have to relocate against your will.

Child: You will experience difficulties in business.

Disabled Person: Misfortunes in business.

Doctor: You are a person of honor and will be recognized as such.

Dwarf: Great danger lies ahead.

Footman: Enemies. You will undertake a journey that could be very dangerous.

Grandparent: A legacy.

Hangman: To see a hangman in your dreams means you will meet with a premature death.

Hermit: A treacherous friend.

Horseman: Pride.

Judge: Punishment. See also Magistrate.

Laborer: Conjugal happiness and increase of fortune.

Lady/Lord: Humiliation.

Lawyer: A friend's marriage.

Locksmith: Robbery.

Lover: Trouble; disputes.

Mayor: Malice.

Millionaire: You will collect on money owed to you from the past; money you had forgotten about.

Money Lender/Banker: Persecution.

Nurse: Long life.

Old Man/Woman: You will be called upon to display your knowledge to others.

Pageboy/Valet: Abuse of confidence.

Painter: Long, happy life.

Pilgrim: You will be justly rewarded.

Police Officer: Apprehension.

Priest: Scandal.

Prince: Honor and profit.

Queen: Prosperity.

Rival: Family quarrels.

Sailor: Tidings from across the sea.

Sculptor: Profit from hard work.

Secretary: Assistance coming.

Shepherd: You will be asked to take on extra responsibilities.

Soldier: Quarrels.

Tailor: Infidelity.

Terrorist: Fear, deep down inside.

Uncle: Advantages.

Waiter/Waitress: Suspicion.

Woodcutter: Hard work for no return.

MELONS: See Fruits.

MERMAID: You will have great expectations followed by big disappointments.

MERRY-GO-ROUND: See Carousel.

MILITARY OFFICER: For a woman to dream of a military officer means she will have many boyfriends. For a man, the dream means that he will achieve recognition in later life.

MILK/MILKING: See Eating/Drinking.

MILLET: See Eating/Drinking.

MILLIONAIRE: Financial success. If you are the millionaire, then you will soon be in a position to help others. See also Meeting.

MIRROR: Betrayal by a friend. A broken mirror signifies that you will be the one betraying a friend.

MISER: If you see a miser counting his gold, it's the best dream you can have. It means you will become rich and prosperous and have a full and happy life.

MIST: See Fog.

MISTLETOE: If you dream that you are being kissed under the mistletoe at Christmas, then when you actually are kissed, that person will become very important in your life. If you dream of a bough of mistletoe falling, it means that you will never marry or, if already married, that you will divorce. If you dream of cutting mistletoe from a tree, then you will have your choice of lovers.

MONASTERY: See Abbey.

MONEY: To give money away means you will lose money in business. To find money means you will have to borrow from others. To receive money as a gift or in payment means you will receive fair recompense for services. See also Alms.

MONEY LENDER/BANKER: See Meeting.

MONKEY: See Ape.

MOON: The moon is tied in with luck and love. To see a full moon means you will be blessed; a new moon means a wish will be granted. A partially clouded moon means you will be lucky in love. To see a moon reflected in water means you will have great expectations, but be disappointed in love. (Interestingly, the Romani word for moon, *shoon*, means "month.")

MOSS: Dreaming of soft, green moss indicates that you are of a loving nature; very affectionate.

MOTORCYCLE: A motorcycle is a powerful vehicle ridden astride. Many see this as a sexual connotation; a warning against reckless sexual encounters. In the present day, it is always wise to be cautious in any sexual encounter, particularly a casual one. But the motorcycle does not have to be connected with sex. Another interpretation is one of controlled power. To ride successfully, one must be in complete control, anticipating every turn. Concentrate on what lies ahead and take control of the throttle and brakes of life. Don't be afraid to open up and speed if the way ahead looks clear.

MOUNTAIN: You have lofty aspirations. If you work hard towards your goal you can achieve it and rise to an important position.

MOURNING: To dream of being in mourning is a reversal of what will actually happen. It means that you will soon have cause for great celebration.

MOUSE/MICE: Dreaming of mice generally means you will experience small, petty annoyances. If you are frightened by a mouse, then you will be very embarrassed over some incident. To see a mouse being chased is a sure sign that you do not stand up for yourself; you let other people push you around. To catch a mouse means you will receive an unpleasant letter. A mouse already caught in a trap is recognition that you have been made to do something you didn't want to do.

MOVIES: See also Television/Video. To be watching a movie is to yearn for glamour in your life. You have been living too sheltered an existence and need to let down your hair a little more. Sometimes the type of movie you are watching can be pertinent:

Comedy: Don't take life too seriously. When you get uptight, examine the situation and try to find a humorous side to it.

Musical: Don't let your love of the music of life cause you to ignore your responsibilities.

Mystery: Something is not as it should be. Don't get complacent, but be always on the alert. Simple, seemingly innocent words and actions can be signs of coming intrigue and complications.

Romance: This could be a good time for romance. Keep your ears and eyes open.

Tragedy: Be aware of tragedies and of impending drama, but always look for the silver lining that will be there somewhere.

War Movie: You are building up to a battle within yourself. Bring your problems out into the open and examine them. Face up to problems and work out solutions.

MUD: This is a symbol of evil that is being directed at you. If you are spattered with mud, then people are maligning you. If you walk or drive through mud, you will come into contact with people who will speak ill of you.

MUFF: See Dress.

MULE: See Ass/Donkey.

MURDER: If you dream of being accused of murder, you will get into an argument with your friends. If you commit a murder, you are refusing to face facts and will get into a difficult situation because of it.

MUSTARD: See Eating/Drinking.

NAKED: See Bare/Naked.

NAPKIN: A fine white napkin indicates that you have a true and faithful friend who will do anything for you. If you drop a napkin, you will do something to hurt that friendship.

NECKLACE: To be wearing an especially fine necklace means that you will be taking part in an important social event. A small, insignificant necklace can mean jealousy and petty annoyances.

NEEDLES: See Dress.

NEGLIGEE/NIGHTGOWN: For a woman to dream that she is dressed in nothing but her negligee means that she has a secret that she is fearful of having discovered.

NEWSPAPER: To buy a newspaper means that you will receive a letter. To be reading a newspaper means that you will get news that could be good or bad, but is more likely to be bad.

NEW YEAR: The Gypsies say that to dream of any aspect of a new year—a New Year's Eve party, being wished a Happy New Year, etc.—indicates that you will have a chance to start afresh, start a new project, implement new ideas, change your course of action, etc.

NIGHTGOWN: See Negligee/Nightgown.

NOVEL: See Library.

NUDE: See Bare/Naked.

NUMBERS: Numbers appearing in dreams are important and you should try hard to remember them, especially if several numbers come together (see Chapter 6, "Dreaming For Profit"). The meanings and associations of individual numbers are as follows:

Zero: Harmony; unity.

One: Solitude; loneliness.

Two: Happiness; the perfect couple.

Three: Dispute; arguments.

Four: Choices; decisions.

Five: Balance.

Six: Exploration; outgoing.

Seven: Luck and blessings.

Eight: New beginnings; new life.

Nine: Family and children.

NUN/NUNNERY: Beware of false friends. See also Convent.

NURSE: You are tired of responsibilities; you need assistance in your business and/or private life. See also Meeting.

NUTS: See Fruits.

OAK TREE: Symbolizes a good, solid marriage. If acorns are falling or have fallen from it, then the marriage will bring many children. See also Acorn.

OAR: To be rowing with two oars means you will forge ahead due to your own efforts. To lose an oar while rowing means you will suffer a minor setback, but will quickly recover.

OATS: A sign of stability and basic success. You will have a firm footing, with a solid business backing.

OBITUARY: To see or read an obituary means a close friend will relocate far away. To read your own obituary means you will be the one relocating.

OFFICERS: Any sort of officer, whether of the law or of one of the armed services, indicates trouble. You will have a brush with the law, or experience trouble through some technicalities, due either to something you have overlooked or something of which you were ignorant. See also Military Officer.

OIL: Generally associated with wealth. To see an oil field signifies that you have money coming. To use an oilcan, buy oil, or pour oil, means you will be well rewarded for your efforts. To spill oil is to lose money.

OLD MAN/WOMAN: See Meeting.

OLIVES: See Fruits.

ONIONS: Different Gypsies have different things to say about onions. Generally they tie in with luck, be it good or bad. If you dream of eating onions, some say you will be a receiver of stolen property, while others say you will discover some hidden treasure. However, many Gypsies say that eating onions means you will get into a very disagreeable argument, perhaps with your own family. To throw away onions means you will break up with your spouse or lover. If you buy onions, you will receive an unexpected bonus.

OPERA: Symbolizes pleasure followed by unhappiness.

OPULENCE: Symbolizes extravagance on your part. Be careful or you will overspend.

ORANGE: See Colors.

ORANGE BLOSSOM: There is peace and tranquility to come . . . but it may not last.

ORANGES: See Fruits.

ORATION: See Speech.

ORCHARD: To dream that you are in an orchard either means that you will become rich by inheriting a good legacy, or that you will marry someone wealthy. For a married person to dream of being in an orchard means there will be many children who, in their turn, will become very wealthy.

ORGAN: To hear organ music or see someone playing the organ means that you will receive very good news. But if the chords should happen to be discordant, then you will receive very bad news.

ORGAN GRINDER/HURDY-GURDY: To see an organ grinder and/or listen to his music indicates that you are being manipulated by somone. If you are working the hurdy-gurdy, then you are the one manipulating.

OVEN: An oven or cooking stove indicates that you will be relocating; moving to a larger home.

OWL: See Bird

OXEN: To see an ox or a yoke of oxen signifies that you will have a hard life with little reward for your pains.

OYSTERS: See Eating/Drinking

PAGEBOY/VALET: See Meeting.

PAINT: To dream of painting a house or putting a fresh coat of paint on anything signifies that you have something to hide; something you are trying to cover up. If someone else is doing the painting, then a friend or associate is hiding something from you.

PAINTER: See Meeting.

PAINTINGS: To see and/or admire fine paintings means that you have many false friends, and that you are wasting a great deal of time.

PALACE: A dream of a palace portends a raising of your standard of living. Beware of living beyond your means.

PALM READER: See Fortunetelling.

PALM TREE: There will be recognition for work you have done and services rendered. The palm tree is a symbol of honor and victory. See also Tree.

PANCAKES: See Eating/Drinking.

PARADISE: To find yourself in what appears to be paradise means you are not being realistic about your work and your surroundings.

PARASOL: To carry a parasol shows that you have many good, close friends. To open a parasol is to receive surprise gifts or advice from these friends.

PARROT: See Bird.

PARTY: See Christmas Party.

PASTRY: See Eating/Drinking.

PATCHWORK: See Quilt.

PAWNSHOP: You are going to be exchanging one set of problems for another.

PEACHES: See Fruits.

PEACOCK: See Bird.

PEARLS: See Dress.

PEARS: See Fruits.

PEN/PENCIL: You will be in a position to make a choice, which will affect a large number of people.

PEPPERMINT: You will be left a sum of money by a distant relative.

PERFUME: If you smell perfume, or apply perfume, you will have a date with a very attractive member of the opposite sex. You will think about becoming romantically involved with him or her.

PHOTOGRAPH: If you dream that you are looking at a photograph of yourself, it is a sign that you will become ill. To look at a photograph of someone else indicates jealousy on your part.

PIANO: To see and hear the piano being played indicates that you will be going to a party. If you are playing the piano, you will be throwing the party.

PICKPOCKET: To dream of a pickpocket shows a need for you to obtain information you are having difficulty getting. If you are the pickpocket, then you are willing to obtain this information illegally if necessary.

PICNIC: You will have a good time with close friends, though there may be a few petty arguments.

PIG: You are assured of success. This is a good time for investing. Whatever you turn your hand to will prosper.

PIGEON: See Bird.

PILGRIM: See Meeting.

PIMPLES: To find your face covered with pimples means that others are very jealous of you.

PINE TREE: Symbolizes an exciting but possibly danger-ous exploit. It could even be an exciting date . . . that you could live to regret!

PINS: See Dress.

PIPE: See Smoke.

PIRATE: You are going to be doing a lot of traveling. Beware of accidents.

PISTOL/REVOLVER: You have an explosive temper. Be careful or you could say something that will hurt some-one and that you will very much regret. See also Gun.

PIT: See Hole.

PITCHFORK: A pitchfork is a sign of excellent health. If you are using a pitchfork, you will be very healthy. If you are chased by someone with a pitchfork, you need to pay more attention to your health.

PLOW: Concentrate on doing your best. Hard work now will lead to great success in the future. This applies both to business and to home life.

PLUMS: See Fruits.

POCKETBOOK/PURSE: To dream of losing a pocketbook means that you are frequently careless and disorganized. To find a pocketbook means that you will have unexpected good fortune.

POLICE: To be arrested by a police officer (or *gavmush*, as the Gypsies say) means that you will do something that will necessitate your apologizing to your friends. To talk with a police officer means that you are in need of advice. See also Meeting and Bailiff/Sheriff.

POMEGRANATE: See Fruits.

PONY: See Horse.

POOL: See Billiards.

POPE: To dream of the pope indicates extravagance. If you dream that you are the pope, then you have been overspending foolishly.

POPPIES: A field of poppies is a sign of adventures in love.

PORCUPINE/HEDGEHOG: Indicates business embarrassments, though some Gypsies say it means a better job but disappointment in friends.

PORT/DOCK: Symbolizes a home or focal point. If you dream of arriving at a dock, you will be going home. To see a ship steam into port similarly indicates that you will be going home, or to the place where you feel most comfortable.

POSTCARD: You will be attending a social event at which you will be very unsure of yourself.

POST OFFICE: You will be meeting with a great many strangers.

POWDER FLASK: Go cautiously, there is some danger should you make the wrong move. See also Gunpowder.

PREACHER: You will encounter a con man.

PRECIPICE: You have a big decision to make. Should you fall down a precipice, you have made a wrong decision!

PRIEST: See Preacher and Meeting.

PRINCE: See Meeting.

PRINTER: You are very much admired for your intelligence and your ease of communication.

PRISON: See Jail.

PROCESSION: Symbolizes constancy in love.

PSYCHIATRIC HOSPITAL: See Asylum.

PUMP: To be at a pump drawing water means that you will have good fortune in business, with money flowing in. If, however, you are pumping and can get no water out, then you will have a failure in your business dealings.

PUNCH/BLOW: To receive a blow or to be hit by a stranger is to learn a valuable lesson. If you are hit by someone you know, then you will be rendered some service.

PURPLE: See Colors.

PURSE: See Pocketbook.

QUARREL: To dream that you are quarreling with someone signifies that you will have advantageous dealings with a business associate. To dream of quarreling with your lover means you will actually draw even closer and will receive a gift from him or her.

QUEEN: See Meeting.

QUILT: To see or handle a quilt is a good sign for financial advances. To be making a quilt shows that you will get good return for the work you have done. A patchwork quilt is a sign of flattery and gossip. Take all you hear with a grain of salt and don't be easily swayed.

RABBIT: See Hare.

RACING: To dream of running a race shows disappointment and anger, especially with your lover. To dream you are riding in a horserace is a sign of good and presages much success in life; you will speedily receive some joyful news, possibly from your lover.

RAGS: To see someone dressed in rags means you have been unfair to someone you really care about. To see yourself dressed in rags means you will come into an inheritance. To dream of handling cleaning rags means you will make money through your own hard work. See also Hobo.

RAILROAD: Signifies security in the long run. You will make slow but steady progress.

RAILROAD ACCIDENT: Your plans will go awry. There will be unexpected pitfalls that will "throw you off the tracks."

RAIN: A gentle shower of rain shows success in your present undertakings. It is especially a good sign for lovers. But if it is heavy rain, with occasional flashes of lightning and rolls of thunder, then beware, for there are going to be many problems and discouragements. See also Lightning and Thunder and Lightning.

RAINBOW: Gypsies believe that if you see a rainbow in your dreams, great happiness will come to you unexpectedly; frequently taking place in the area of love.

RAKE: To dream of a garden rake indicates that you need to get your plans better organized. You cannot progress until you have a clearer understanding of where you want to go.

RAM: This animal indicates that you are trying to force the issue. You need to relax and let things move under their own steam for a while.

RAT: You have a secret enemy who is working against you. Someone who appears to be a friend (though not a close one) is really an enemy. He or she is not so much plotting against you, but is learning your secrets to use to his or her advantage.

RAVEN: See Bird.

REAPER: See Scythe.

RED: See Colors.

REPTILE: Someone you are not sure about is actually a very good friend who will work for your well-being. Given recognition, this person will turn out to be the best friend you have ever had.

RETIREMENT: To dream of retiring indicates a need for a vacation. You have been working for too long without a break. Give yourself a well-deserved rest.

REVOLVER: See Pistol.

RIBBONS: See Dress.

RICE: See Eating/Drinking.

RING: Approaching marriage.

RING (JEWELED): A cheap, flashy ring means you will have a minor ailment. A rich, expensive ring means you will be robust, with excellent health.

RIOT: To dream that you witness of or are engaged in a riot means that you will get unexpected news and an unexpected visitor. It can also mean that the object of your affections is wavering between you and another suitor.

RIVAL: See Meeting.

RIVER: To dream you see a flowing river whose waters are smooth and clear presages happiness and success in life; for the married person, contentment in family life. If the waters of the river are rough and muddy, you will be taking a journey that could lead to an increase in your fortunes, though there are certain risks attached.

ROAD: The Rom say that a wide, straight road indicates you will find things coming to you very easily, without too much effort on your part. If the road is winding, with ups and downs, then that is how you will find life: many ups and downs and changes of fortune along the way.

ROAST: Eating/Drinking.

ROCK: An obstruction; an annoyance. Note how you get around or over the rock in your dream. A falling rock indicates an unexpected change of fortune.

ROCKING CHAIR: To see someone, or yourself, rocking in a chair is a sign that you will have an easy, contented life. To rock an empty chair means that there will be many hard times.

ROPE: To see and/or handle rope signifies you will be in a position to make several very useful friends. If there are knots in the rope, you will have a few problems but will overcome them. If you cut a rope, you will sever what could be a very useful relationship.

ROSE: Always a happy omen, according to the Gypsies. A full-bloom rose indicates health, joy, and happiness. A rose bud signifies the potential for a wonderful friendship to develop. A faded rose means you are neglecting an old friend. A white rose shows innocence; a red rose, satisfaction.

RUBY: Strong, romantic love, though it may be fleeting.

RUG: See Carpet.

RUNNING: To be running in your dream means that time is passing, and you need to act quickly or you will miss an opportunity.

SADDLE: You will have ease and comfort in life.

SAILOR: Indicative of journeys. You may be relocating or it may just be a journey away and back home again. See also Meeting.

SALAD: See Eating/Drinking.

SALT: See Eating/Drinking.

SAND: Indicates a coming increase in finances. Investments will bring good returns, but beware that the new-found money is not as quickly washed away again.

SANDALS: To be wearing sandals is a sign of success. If the sandals hurt your feet, you will have many problems but will eventually overcome them all.

SATIN: See Dress.

SAUSAGES: See Eating/Drinking.

SCARAB: The Egyptian scarab is a sacred beetle and, in a dream, indicates that you are on the right path. If you continue working as industriously as you have been, it will lead to rich rewards.

SCARE: To dream you are scared by some frightening object or event shows that you have many reservations about a decision you have recently made. You need to examine that decision.

SCISSORS: Enemies. Hatred.

SCULPTOR: See Meeting.

SCYTHE: A symbol for cutting back or ending. If you are the one with the scythe, then you feel the need to cut back on something, or put an end to an action or situation. If you see the "Grim Reaper"— a robed or unrobed skeletal figure with a scythe—it does not necessarily mean death. It could indicate a death to come, but it could just as easily indicate the coming end of a job, situation, relationship, or whatever. Don't forget that where there are endings there are new beginnings, and therefore, new opportunities.

SEA: A long journey. A calm sea means that it will be a successful and enjoyable journey. A rough sea indicates many problems and worries.

SEAL: A single seal or a group of seals indicates that you will be going on a fishing trip.

SEALING WAX: You will receive the approval you have been waiting for to go ahead with what you have planned.

SEAWEED: Someone is trying to prevent you from taking a journey that would prove beneficial for you.

SECRETARY: See Meeting.

SERMON: If you are listening to a sermon, you will receive some good advice from a friend. You will be wise to follow it. If you are delivering a sermon, you will be accused of double-crossing someone.

SERPENT: See Reptile.

SHADOWS: Strong shadows in your dreams indicate pessimism and the possibility of failure. However bright your prospects seem, you will still be conscious of the fact that things could go terribly wrong.

SHAMROCK: You will have a wonderful time with someone you admire very much.

SHARK: Danger from jealous enemies. Do not be panicked into doing anything without careful thought.

SHAVING: To dream of shaving means you tend to be miserly. To cut yourself while shaving means you are going to lose money through your unwillingness to speculate.

SHAWL: Gypsies say it symbolizes solace and comfort.

SHEEP: Slow and steady progress. To shear a sheep means a profit in business. Herding sheep means you are worried about a close friend's actions.

SHEPHERD: See Meeting.

SHERIFF: See Bailiff.

SHIP: See Boat.

SHIPWRECK: You will suffer a dangerous illness, but it will not prove fatal.

SHIRT: To take off a shirt means you will lose a friend. To lose a button off a shirt means petty squabbles. To wear a bright, clean shirt means happiness to come.

SHOES: See Boots.

SHOOTING: To dream of shooting means you are ready to act; to go ahead with something you have been brooding about for a long time. To hunt and shoot with a bow and arrow means you will be taking a big chance, but the risk could pay off very well. See also Arrow and Gun.

SILK: See Dress.

SILVER: Silver money and ingots indicate honors and prestige that will come to you. The Rom say that to dream of silverware on a dining table means you will receive unwelcome visitors in your home.

SINGING: To be singing with others means you will enjoy meeting with old friends. To sing solo means you will find yourself alone.

SKELETON: You will be involved in some unusual activities. If a skeleton with a scythe, see Scythe.

SKULL: You will make a big discovery that could greatly benefit you.

SMOKE: If you see smoke from a chimney or fire, you will enjoy a brief moment of joy, but it will not last. To smoke a cigarette or pipe indicates that you have great confidence in yourself, which may or may not be justified. See also Chimney.

SNAIL: You seem to be making slow and steady progress, but if you stop to examine things, you will find you are going in the wrong direction.

SNAKE: See Reptile.

SNOW: Light snow falling is a sign of contentment. Heavy snow is a warning to exercise caution. To see snow weighting down branches of trees means you are under pressure to produce. Children playing in the snow means you will be justly rewarded.

SOLDIER: Be prepared for troubles to come. To see a number of soldiers means more and bigger troubles. See also Meeting.

SOUP: See Eating/Drinking.

SPEECH: To be listening to a speech means that you will shortly have an opportunity to learn things which can be of great benefit to you. If you are delivering a speech, you will be in a position to help someone who will appreciate your assistance.

SPEEDING TICKET: You are being too hasty! Slow down and think about what you are doing. Don't rush to judgment. Don't make decisions without first writing out all the pros and cons and giving them due consideration.

SPIDER: To dream of spiders is lucky. They symbolize luck and great prosperity through industry. You will soon achieve your ambition. If the spider is on a web, then the good fortune will come from a number of different sources. See also Cobweb.

SPORTS: Dreams of spectator sports reflect the mass hysteria often found in life. If you have a decision to make, be sure that it is your own decision and not just reflecting the general feelings of those around you, even if it means having to go against those general feelings.

Playing sports can have different meanings for the type of sport involved:

Baseball: If pitching, you are in a position to position things the way you want them. It is up to you how you "throw the ball." If batting, you are about to face an onslaught—be it a decision to be made, a face-off with an opponent, or dealing with a group of people. If fielding, you must keep your eyes open for anything driven your way, so that you may deal with it appropriately.

Football: You are in the middle of a challenging game where people can come at you from any and all ways. You could get hurt, but not if you keep on your toes and are ready to move quickly at the slightest opportunity that presents itself.

Soccer: You literally need to keep on your toes and be ready with some fancy footwork, if necessary. Be ready to dodge opponents and shoot for the goal as soon as you see the opportunity.

Tennis: You have an opponent or two who is out to beat you. You are evenly matched and, if you think as you act, you can win. Don't be tricked into running the wrong way.

SQUIRREL: A squirrel storing nuts means that you will enjoy social success. But a squirrel chasing through the branches of a tree means debtors will be after you.

STAG: Represents eventual financial and social gain. To see a stag killed means there will be a scandal. If you are the one who kills the stag, you will be the center of a scandal. See also Deer.

STARS: Bright stars in the sky mean recovery from an illness. A shooting star signifies the birth of a baby.

STEAMBOAT: Unexpected news from afar.

STEEPLE: You will meet an interesting person of the opposite sex. Carefully check out him or her before becoming involved.

STORK: Foretells a robbery.

STRAWBERRIES: See Fruits.

STREAM: See Brook.

STRESS/ANXIETY: A warning to the physical from the mental that you are approaching a breakdown. You need to make a change as soon as possible; either a change of job or a change of attitude to the job. If the stress and anxiety is related to a relationship rather than a job situation, then you need to distance yourself (if only temporarily) from the person causing the conflict.

SUNRISE/SUNSET: A beautiful sunrise presages success in a new venture. A beautiful sunset tells of rewards to come from work already done.

SWALLOW: See Bird.

SWAN: See Bird.

SWEEP (CHIMNEY): You will acquire a store of very useful knowledge—a piece here, a piece there— which you will suddenly realize can be put together and used for your profit.

SWEEPING: To be sweeping with a broom means that you need to clear out all the smaller, accumulated bits and pieces of your life and concentrate on the more important things, claim Gypsies in the southwest of England.

SWIMMING: To dream of swimming with your head above water means you will have good success. To swim with your head under the water means you will be weighed down with problems. To swim in the nude means you will enjoy social successes.

SWORD: To hold a sword, wear one, or brandish one means you will be awarded some special recognition. To be fighting with a sword means you will quarrel with business associates.

SYCAMORE: To dream of the sycamore tree means there is jealousy in your marriage or love affair. See also Tree.

TAILOR: You are going to be very busy with little time to enjoy yourself. See also Meeting.

TAMBOURINE: If you play a tambourine, you are going to be held accountable for your actions . . . and are not too happy at the prospects! If you watch someone else playing a tambourine, you will be in a position to call someone to account for their actions.

TANDEM: To dream of a tandem bicycle means you will be going into partnership, either in business or by getting married.

TATTOO: You will never be able to keep any secret to yourself.

TAXI: See Cab.

TEA: If you dream that you are pouring tea for someone, it means you will be approached for a loan. To dream of drinking tea with someone is a sign that that person is good and trustworthy.

TEARS: To dream that you are in tears means that you will receive a letter containing bad news. If you see a baby crying, it is a sign that the letter will have good news.

TELESCOPE: You will be traveling to a far distant place that you will find interesting and exciting.

TELEVISION/VIDEO: If you are watching a video or television movie and are able to follow the story, note that the main character in the movie represents yourself. Whatever sort of program you are watching, if you are able to follow it in your dream, it relates to you and your present problems or situation. Relate it to the universal and personal symbolism given in the earlier part of this book. If you are unable to choose which video to play, you need to examine your choices in life or work and give good thought to where you want to go.

TENT: A Gypsy tent is known as a *bender*. To dream of sleeping in a tent is to feel safe and secure. To dream that you are erecting a tent means you are working well towards your own security.

TERRORIST: See Meeting.

THEATER: To be at a theater, moviehouse, or watching a play, means you will attend a social event but will feel out of place there.

THIRST: To dream you have an unquenchable thirst signifies that you seek new knowledge; you are looking for an answer to a longterm problem.

THISTLE: You are attracted to someone who could hurt you, though not seriously.

THORNS: Dreaming of thorns means you are stepping on dangerous ground. You could suffer greatly if you rush on without thinking of where you are going, so plan ahead as thoroughly and carefully as you can.

THUNDER AND LIGHTNING: Rough times ahead with much dispute, arguments, disagreement, possibly even law suits. If you hear thunder without seeing lightning, then you will come out of it all right. See also Lightning and Rain.

TIGER: Fierce enmity; animosity towards a particular person. To hunt a tiger means that a trap has been laid for you but you will recognize it and avoid it. To kill a tiger means triumph over your enemies.

TINKER: To dream that you are a tinker mending pots and pans means that you will be prosperous in business, successful as a lover, and happy and contented when married.

TOAD: To dream of a toad indicates the possibility of an accident. To pick up a toad means a minor aggravation, such as a cut finger or stubbed toe.

TOMB: To enter a tomb means you will suffer an illness. To be locked in a tomb means it will be a very serious illness.

TORCH: To dream of carrying a lighted torch symbolizes troubles to come in your love life. To extinguish a torch means you will break with your present lover.

TORTOISE: See Turtle.

TRAIN: To see a train going by is a sign of missed opportunity. To be riding on a train means you will achieve goals even though you don't work especially hard towards them. A freight train is indicative of manual labor, while a passenger train points to mental work. See also Engine.

TRAMP: See Hobo.

TRAVELING: Frequently symbolizing spiritual progression, though the Gypsies are usually not especially aware of this. For them to dream of traveling, in whatever form, is a natural progression of life; advancement, goals attained, new friends, and situations.

TRAY: To dream of holding a tray indicates that you will be supporting someone, either financially or morally. To drop a tray is to let down a friend.

TREASURE: To hunt for treasure is to seek recognition. To discover buried or sunken treasure is to receive an unexpected award or recognition.

TREE: A tree symbolizes strength and beauty to the Gypsies. To see a number of trees or a woods is to know that you will have many children who will grow up tall and strong. To dream of cutting down a tree means that you will harm yourself. To see a leafless tree means that you will suffer sickness. Climbing a tree signifies excelling in your field. To break a branch from a tree is a falling-out with your lover. See also individual tree names.

TRIPLETS: A sign of good luck, good health, wealth, and abundance.

TROMBONE: To play a trombone or see or hear one being played signifies success in love.

TRUMPET: To play a trumpet or see or hear one being played signifies a mild flirtation, which could develop into something serious.

TULIPS: To dream of these flowers is a sign of abundance. If you see yourself standing in a garden surrounded by tulips, it foretells that you will be rich and distinguished.

TUNNEL: To dream of going through a lighted tunnel denotes that you will successfully negotiate your way through one or more difficult times—possibly business dealings or domestic problems—while going through a dark tunnel means you will have a really hard time along the way.

TURKEY: A live turkey means you will be asked to make a speech. A dead or cooked turkey forebodes involvement in a scandal.

TURNIP: To dream of being in a turnip field denotes acquisition of riches; to the lover they augur great fidelity and good temper in your sweetheart.

TURTLE/TORTOISE: Symbolizes delays and vexations in business affairs.

ULCERS: To dream that you have ulcers is to acknowledge that you are greatly concerned about something; worrying more than you should. Try to relax and bring your worries and fears out into the open or you may well develop real ulcers.

UMBRELLA: Carrying an umbrella in your dreams indicates that you feel vulnerable and in need of protection. This is doubly so if you have an open umbrella. See also Parasol.

UNCLE/AUNT: To see them in your dreams is a sign of upcoming family quarrels. See also Meeting.

UNDERCLOTHING: To dream you are not wearing underwear means you are afraid of being found out in a lie; you have something to hide. To be wearing torn underclothing means you are ashamed of some recent action of yours.

UNDERTAKER: To meet with an undertaker in your dreams is to anticipate such a meeting in real life. Someone you know, but not related to you, will soon die, and you will attend the funeral.

URGENCY: If there is great urgency in your own or someone else's actions, it is a sign that you are very impatient.

VALET: See Meeting (Pageboy).

VALLEY: All Gypsies seem to agree that to be walking in a valley is a sign of contentment and tranquility, and a knowledge of protection.

VAULT: A bank vault is a sign of hidden riches. You are trying to obtain something, but being frustrated in its acquisition. A bank vault with an open door is a sign that you are giving away too many secrets; talking too much.

VARDO: See Carriage.

VEIL: See Dress.

VELVET: See Dress.

VENUS: For a young man to dream of the goddess Venus signifies that he is seeking the ideal woman. For a young woman to dream of the lady means that she is feeling sexually frustrated.

VINEGAR: See Eating/Drinking.

VINEYARD: A full vineyard, with many bunches of rich purple grapes, symbolizes a life of riches and good fortune. Green, unripe grapes on the vines indicate the potential for riches, but you will have to work at it.

VIOLIN: The *bosh* is a favorite instrument of the Gypsies. To dream that you see and/or hear one being played is a very good sign, symbolizing much enjoyment and good company. To dream that you are playing the bosh is to know that you are much loved and admired.

VIRGIN: For a woman to dream she is a virgin is to wish to be desirable to men. For a man to dream of a virgin is to desire a younger woman.

VIXEN: A vixen is a symbol for a mixture of beauty and cunning. Beware of any especially beautiful, self-assured woman who seems to attract you.

VULTURE: See Bird.

WAGON: See Carriage.

WAITER/WAITRESS: See Meeting.

WAR: To dream of a war being fought indicates that there will be a great scandal in which you will play a prominent part!

WARMING PAN: To dream of a warming pan indicates that you will be going to bed with a stranger.

WASP: Wasps are signs of trouble with envious people. To be stung by a wasp means you will spend money foolishly. See also Insects.

WATCH: To be wearing a watch or to consult a watch means you will be visited by a very important person.

WATCH (GOLD): You will receive some public recognition.

WATER: Clear, cold water is a sign of good health. Warm or dirty water indicates illness. To empty water out of a vessel shows you have an unhealthy appetite and need to watch what you eat.

WATERFALL: A sign that you will meet with many new and interesting people who will like you.

WATERMILL: You will have continuing good health and a steady income, with little change over many years.

WEALTH: What you dream you have in wealth you lack in health. If you dream you are very rich, then you need to pay a lot of attention to your health.

WEASEL: Cunning and deceit.

WEDDING: Attending a wedding means you will meet new friends. If it is your own wedding, you will be extremely fortunate in love. See also Interracial Marriage.

WEEDS: To see a garden filled with weeds means that you need to review your diet and health; for if you continue as you are, you will become extremely sick.

WEEPING: See Tears.

WELL: To draw water from a well means that you will meet with a stranger who will provide you with much useful information.

WHEAT: A field of ripe wheat indicates that you will grow rich. If the wheat has already been harvested, you will just miss a wonderful opportunity to make a lot of money (such as being close to the winning number in a lottery).

WHEELS: When turning wheels are emphasized in a dream, it indicates travel. If the wheels are stationary, you will be making some short trips.

WHIP: To use a whip or see a whip being used indicates that you have a short temper and sharp tongue that can hurt others more than you realize.

WHIRLPOOL: You are in a very dangerous situation and could be swept away, without warning, at any time.

WHIRLWIND: You will get into a tremendous argument with a relative and say things that you will later regret.

WIDOW: For a woman to dream that she is a widow means that her lover is being unfaithful.

WIG: To dream of wearing a wig means you are being pretentious or allowing people to believe things of you that are not true.

WILL: To dream that you are writing your will means that you are very dissatisfied with the actions of some close relative(s).

WINDMILL: If the sails of the windmill are turning, then you will enjoy a large inheritance. If they are at a standstill, then the inheritance will be small.

WOLF: Symbolizes strength and independence.

WOMAN (BEAUTIFUL): Success in love and/or business. Recognition for your efforts.

WOOD: See Tree.

WOODCUTTER: See Meeting.

WORK: See Job.

WORM: To dream of worms is a warning that you may be in contact with someone who has a contagious disease.

WRECK: A wreck at sea is a sign of a tedious and costly lawsuit, which could lead to poverty and even imprisonment.

WRITING DESK: To be sitting at a writing desk signifies that your words will carry a lot of weight; what you say will have an effect on many people. See also Desk.

YACHT: To see a yacht go sailing by means you will become friendly with a person who is wealthy. If you are sailing the yacht, you will become wealthy yourself. See also Boat.

YARN: A ball of yarn signals the start of a long, winding affair, either business or of the heart.

YELLOW: See Colors.

YEW TREE: A symbol of strength. You are someone others can lean on when they have a need. Your friends find that they can turn to you with their problems. See also Tree.

YOKE: See Oxen.

ZEBRA: Some Gypsies say this indicates misplaced friendship. Others say it simply means there are two equally important sides to a problem under consideration; either choice could be right.

ZODIAC: To dream of the zodiac as a whole shows a great interest in your fellow humans; an inquiring and active mind. To dream of any particular sign, you must consider the general astrological meanings. The common Romani interpretations are as follows:

Aries: Leader; pioneer. Sometimes impatient and overly ambitious.

Taurus: Hard worker. Great strength (and proud of it); perseverence.

Gemini: Adaptable. Knows a little about a lot of things. Gift for languages.

Cancer: Extremely sensitive. Homelover. Follower of tradition.

Leo: Extrovert. Sense of the dramatic. Great lover.

Virgo: Conservative. Critical; analytical. Best of planners or organizers. Intellectual.

Libra: Has intuition and foresight. Peace loving, with great sense of justice.

Scorpio: Has tenacity and determination. Great self-control but too fine an opinion of self. Can be jealous and demanding.

Sagittarius: Knows no fear. Kind and gentle, yet out spoken and direct.

Capricorn: Ambitious; materialistic. Fear of inadequacy. Can be greatly depressed or incredibly happy.

Aquarius: The planner; always looking ahead. Independent. Honest and kind, but difficult to understand.

Pisces: Sensitive; noble. Can be vague and overly optimistic. Excellent diplomat.

The Gypsies connect the parts of the body with the signs as follows: head—Aries; neck—Taurus; arms—Gemini; breast—Cancer; heart—Leo; bowels—Virgo; kidneys—Libra; genitalia—Scorpio; thighs—Sagittarrius; knees—Capricorn; legs—Aquarius; feet—Pisces. So if you dream of, for example, the sign Capricorn, it could be because of a problem you have with your knee(s) and/or indicative of feelings of inadequacy.

Index